Teresa Weatherspoon's
Basketball
for Girls

● ● ● ●

Teresa Weatherspoon's
Basketball
for Girls

Teresa Weatherspoon
with Tara Sullivan
and Kelly Whiteside

John Wiley & Sons, Inc.

New York ● Chichester ● Weinheim ● Brisbane ● Singapore ● Toronto

Copyright © 1999 by Mountain Lion, Inc., and Teresa Weatherspoon. All rights reserved

Published by John Wiley & Sons, Inc.
Published simultaneously in Canada

Design and production by Navta Associates, Inc.

The logos, emblems, team names and other insignia of the WNBA and its teams are trademarks and copyrighted designs and other forms of intellectual property owned by WNBA Enterprises, LLC and are used herein with the permission of WNBA Enterprises, LLC. WNBA Enterprises, LLC disclaims responsibility for the truth and accuracy of all statements contained within this text, and the opinions expressed within this text do not represent the opinions of WNBA Enterprises, LLC.

The publisher and the author have made every reasonable effort to ensure that the experiments and activities in this book are safe when conducted as instructed but assume no responsibility for any damage caused or sustained while performing the experiments or activities in the book. Parents, guardians, and/or teachers should supervise young readers who undertake the experiments and activities in this book.

Library of Congress Cataloging-in-Publication Data:
Weatherspoon, Teresa
      Teresa Weatherspoon's basketball for girls / Teresa Weatherspoon with Tara Sullivan and Kelly Whiteside.
            p.   cm.
      Summary: Provides instruction and advice for young women who want to play basketball, covering dribbling, passing, shooting and rebounding, as well as individual and team offense and defense.
      ISBN 0-471-31784-5 (alk. paper)
      1. Basketball for girls—Juvenile literature. [1. Basketball for girls.] I. Sullivan, Tara. II. Whiteside, Kelly. III. Title. IV. Title: Basketball for girls.
      GV886.W43   1999
      796.323 082—dc21   98–45160
                                                                                                         CIP

Printed in the United States of America
10 9 8 7 6 5 4 3 2 1

Acknowledgments

First, I'd like to give all the Honor, Glory and Praise to God.
I Thank You, I Love You and I Adore You.

Special thanks to my family:

Rowena Weatherspoon
Charles Weatherspoon Sr.
Charles Weatherspoon Jr. and Bernadette
Diana Weatherspoon
Carolyn Weatherspoon
Michael Weatherspoon
Denise Weatherspoon
Anthony Weatherspoon
Dominique Weatherspoon
Tanaya Weatherspoon
Brandon Weatherspoon
Jalen Weatherspoon

You are all the reason for *many things* that happen in my life. I love you all soooo much. Hugs and kisses 4-ever.

Many thanks also to:

Paris—you are very dear to me—thanks for your advice, *your help,* and for just being the unique person that you are—you're always in my heart.

Oscar—you know how important you are.

Bruce Levy Associates International, Ltd.—Bruce, Erica, Evan, and Jenn—smile, there's more to come.

Randy Voorhees and the Mountain Lion, Inc., staff, along with Kate Bradford and the John Wiley & Sons staff—thank you for the opportunity.

Tara Sullivan

Kelly Whiteside

Christ the King High School basketball team and staff

Retha Swindell

Coach Leon Barmore

Carol Blazejowski and the entire New York Liberty organization

The Women's Sports Foundation

All my friends, you know who you are. I love you.

Tyra Banks, Gregory Hines, Rosie O'Donnell, and Dr. Bill Cosby—thank you for your continued support.

Big shout-outs to the Liberty Sistas:

Vickie Johnson ("VJ")

Sophia Witherspoon ("So So")

Kym Hampton ("Big Hamp")

Rebecca Lobo ("B")

Kisha Ford ("Kee")

Coquese Washington ("Little One")

Trena Trice ("T^2")

Elisabeth Cebrian ("Bettie")

Alicia Thompson ("Chelle")

Sue Wicks ("Warrior")

The Liberty coaching staff

You are all *simply amazing!* Much love!

Last but not least, thank you to the fans of New York. *You are the best*—continue to support us, because we're coming *BACK!*

Please, please forgive me if I left anyone out, anybody. Trust me, you are *appreciated. MUCH LOVE!!*

Spoon

Contents

Introduction

This book is for girls all over the world who love to play basketball. When I was young, I didn't have professional women athletes to look up to or to pattern myself after. I had to watch the men play. But now there are so many more opportunities for women in sports, and I want to let girls know that they can make their dreams come true, just like I did. I want girls to be able to look up to me, and I want to share what I know about this game of basketball that I love so much.

I hope that you will learn a lot from this book, mostly about skills and ways to make yourself a better player. I give you ideas on every facet of the game, and in many chapters there are drills to help you improve. But more than anything, I hope you will learn about my passion for the game. Even though I play professional basketball for the New York Liberty of the WNBA, basketball is more than a job for me, it is my love. Like anybody who wants to be the best at what they do, I want to be the best basketball player on any court. I hope that through reading about my career, my family, my youth, my high school and college days, and, of course, my pro career in the WNBA, you will see for yourself how you can achieve your dreams.

Keep this book nearby and check back with it often. If you have a tough practice or a tough shooting night in a game, come back and read about when that happened to me. Remember that I had tough times, too, and they made me stronger. And when you find a certain aspect of your game lagging, check back with the ideas here. Make sure you are preparing yourself the right way for a game.

To parents and coaches, I hope that you, too, will find this book useful. You are such important individuals in the lives of young people. I was lucky that I had wonderful role models in my mom, Rowena, and my college coach at Louisiana Tech, Leon Barmore. You also can become important shapers of young lives if you approach the game the right way. Don't pressure the kids to do too much; let them enjoy the game, see its beauty, and most of all, let them have fun playing it. Clearly the odds are against most kids becoming professional athletes. But the benefits of playing basketball—learning to work with teammates, to deal with satisfaction and disappointment—will be important in every girl's life.

The first step in any new venture is just that: taking a step. If you have never played basketball before or if you have just decided to start playing more seriously, congratulations. I hope reading what I have done to become a good player will help you reach your goal. Don't be afraid to start. A journey of a thousand miles begins with one step. That's all it takes. Join in.

1

Before
You Start

Warming Up

When I get to the gym, I can't wait to start playing, but I resist the temptation and always warm up first. Why is it important? Because warming up and stretching help keep your body injury-free. Always warm up your body for about five minutes before beginning any stretches to avoid injury. To begin your warm-up, jog around the court three times. Then stand with your arms out by your sides and make small circles, five to the front and five to the back. Increase the size of the circles and do five more in one direction and five more in the other. Now your muscles are warm before you stretch.

Stretching

Remember to stretch before every practice and game. Actually, I stretch after each game and practice, too. It's a good habit to get into. The following routine stretches the major parts of your body that you use the most when playing basketball. The best way to stretch is *slooooowly*. Bouncing while stretching can cause injury because your muscles will tighten, not relax. Your body needs time to loosen up each of the muscle groups before you can perform at your best. A few guidelines: Go lightly, holding your stretch for about ten to twenty seconds. Relax after each stretch for about twenty seconds. Do each stretch two or three times. Each time try to extend the stretch a bit farther. There never should be pain. If there is, you're forcing the stretch too much.

Here are some simple stretches to help you get loose before a game or practice.

The lower leg stretch works your calf muscles and hamstring tendon.

Lower Leg Stretch

Sit on the floor with one leg straight and the other positioned so the heel of your sneaker touches the inside of your opposite thigh. Bend forward at the waist and grab the ankle or foot of your straight leg. Hold for twenty seconds. Repeat on opposite leg.

Hurdler Stretch

Still seated, spread your legs to form a V. With your left hand, reach out and touch your right ankle or toe. Hold that position for twenty seconds. Then repeat the process with the right hand touching your left ankle or toe.

Butterflies

Still seated, put your heels together in front of you and pull your feet close to your body. (Your legs will look like the wings of a butterfly.) Grab your right ankle with your right hand and your left ankle with your left hand. Put light pressure on your knees with your elbows and push forward slowly. Hold for twenty seconds.

Standing Groin Stretch

Stand and spread your feet a little more than shoulder width apart so you feel a slight pull in your groin and hamstring muscles. Bend over and try to put both hands on the floor. Hold for twenty seconds.

The butterfly stretch works your groin area and the large muscles in your thigh.

Side Lunge Stretch

Take the same position but this time lean to the left, bending your left leg and keeping your right leg straight. Hold for twenty seconds, then repeat on the other side.

The side lunge stretch works the hamstring tendon in the hollow of your knee.

The front lunge stretch works the large quadriceps muscle at the front of your thigh.

Front Lunge Stretch

Facing forward, bend your left leg and keep your right leg extended behind you. Put both your forearms on top of your left thigh. Keep your chest upright. Hold for twenty seconds, then repeat on the other side.

Calf Stretch

Stand a few feet from a wall and put one foot in front of the other. Keep your heels flat on the floor and lean forward against the wall. Hold for twenty seconds, then repeat with the other foot forward.

Trunk Twists

Standing with your feet spread apart, twist your upper body left and right, holding your arms at chest level.

Flamingo Stretch

Standing, grab your right foot with your right hand and pull it behind your right leg to your buttocks. (Sometimes it's hard to balance while standing on one leg, so grab a wall or a teammate's shoulder until you get the hang of it.) Hold for twenty seconds. Repeat with the left foot.

The flamingo stretch works the large quadriceps muscle at the front of your thigh.

Triceps Stretch

Standing, hold your left elbow over your head with your right hand. (Your left elbow should be above your left ear.) Pull your elbow behind your head. Hold for about twenty seconds. Repeat with your right elbow.

Biceps-Shoulder Stretch

Standing, pull your right arm across your chest and hook it with your left elbow until you feel a stretch. Hold for about twenty seconds. Repeat with your left arm.

The triceps stretch works the triceps muscle at the back of your upper arm.

The biceps-shoulder stretch works the muscles in your shoulder and the large biceps muscle in the front of your upper arm.

Spoon Servings

Full name: Teresa Gaye Weatherspoon

Nickname: Spoon

Height/Weight: 5'8", 161 lbs.

Birthdate: December 8, 1965

Birthplace: Jasper, Texas

Home: New York City and Pineland, Texas

High school: West Sabine High School (Pineland, Texas)

College: Louisiana Tech, '88

Years of pro basketball: 10

Sports I like to play (other than basketball): Softball

Athlete I most admired as a kid: Muhammad Ali because he was an honest man, whether you liked what he had to say or not

Favorite food: Pasta, any kind of way

Favorite color: Dark blue

Biggest sports thrill: Winning the 1988 NCAA Championship

Runner-up: Hitting a shot as a freshman at LA Tech to send the game into overtime against USC and Hall-of-Famer-to-be Cheryl Miller

Proudest moment: Receiving the Wade Trophy in 1988 after Coach Leon Barmore pushed me to be the best I could be

Place I like to be when not playing: Pineland. I love to be at home. I like being around my nephews and nieces, watching them grow.

Number: I wear No. 11 in memory of a favorite uncle who passed away on my eleventh birthday. I also wear eleven braids in my hair at all times.

Music: R&B, soft soothing music. Nothing that would tear my ears off.

Favorite subjects in school: Math and English

Pet: A cocker spaniel named Magic

Hidden talent: No one knows that I can do karate. My dad put me in classes as a kid.

Game day routine: I eat a banana about an hour before the game. It gives me an energy spurt.

Favorite quote: "Your life is successful when you have an impact on another life." —Jackie Robinson

Best advice ever received: My mother always said, "Believe. Times are hard, but believe." If my team is down by twenty, I still believe. You will never see me giving up.

Warm-up Drills

Now that your muscles are warm, you can do a few drills to further get your body ready. These drills will not only get you loose, they'll help improve your speed and endurance, making you a better player.

Suicide Drill

As you can guess from the name, this drill is never fun, but it is always useful. Because a basketball game is a series of quick bursts, it's good to do some sprints that focus on changing directions. Line up at the baseline and sprint to the nearest free-throw line; then run back to the baseline. Then sprint to half-court and back. Next, sprint to the far free-throw line and back. Finally, sprint to the far baseline and back. Three sets of these are a good start.

Jumping Drill

Jumping is crucial in basketball, so it's important to practice. This drill will help you jump higher. Stand next to a wall with a piece of chalk in your hand (be sure it's a wall where a chalk mark won't matter). Hold the chalk high and jump into the air, making a mark as high as you can. Then do ten more jumps, and make sure that each one is at least as high as your first chalk mark.

Line Jumps

This drill will help you develop coordination as well as get your legs ready to take all the jumping you'll have to do in a game. Stand with both feet together on one side of a straight line (the baseline, sideline, or whatever) and jump into the air across the line while keeping both feet together. Do this for thirty seconds, back and forth.

Line jumps get your heart pumping, develop coordination, and prepare the leg muscles for the jumping that takes place during a basketball practice or game.

The Olympics

In 1988 we won the gold medal. My teammates were crying, but I didn't know how to react. I don't think that what winning the gold really meant hit me until 1992. When we won the bronze that year, I dropped my head and walked away. I didn't even want to touch that bronze medal. I saw the bronze as a prize for being a failure. But then I realized that when I walked away with my head down, I embarrassed myself. I understood that the Olympics are about more than winning it all. They're about competing, playing for your country. I fought for my country, played as hard as I could for my country. That means a lot to me. Now I cherish the bronze medal as much as the gold medal.

2

Dribbling

et's begin by discussing the role dribbling plays in basketball. There are two main reasons to use the dribble: to control the ball and to advance the ball up and down the court. Many players start dribbling the second they get the ball, but this is not always wise. Of the three options when you receive the basketball—dribble, pass, or shoot—dribbling should be your third choice, because once you use it up it's gone. Once you start to dribble, you have to keep doing it until you either pass or shoot. When you stop, you are not allowed to start dribbling again. If you stop bouncing with neither the shot or pass available, the defense can trap you and easily steal the ball.

Dribbling is a vital skill to successful basketball. This is especially true for guards, who need to be able to control the ball and create opportunities for their teammates. First, we will take a look at how to use the dribble to control the ball.

The Control Dribble

The control dribble is the first dribble that any player should learn. It is the way to maintain possession of the ball, to keep it away from a defender, to take time off the clock, and to get in better position to make a pass or take a shot. What is the control dribble all about? One way of answering that is to realize what it is not. It's not for showing off how good you are. It's not what you should do just because you're not sure what else to do with the ball. A dribble without a purpose is an open invitation for your defender to strip away the ball. So think before you bounce. Don't put the ball on the floor until and unless you know what you're going to do with it.

What is the proper way to dribble? The control dribble can be broken down into several simple steps.

Begin Slowly

Start with your fingertips on the ball and your hand cupped. Don't slap at the ball with your palm; it will only make you lose control. Touch the ball with only one hand at a time; if you bounce with two hands you will be called for *double dribbling* and the other team will get the ball. And remember, any time you move on the court with the ball, you must be dribbling. If you take steps without bouncing the ball, you will be called for *traveling* and, again, the other team will get the ball.

Keep Your Body Loose

A stiff approach will not work here; you need to loosen up to be a good dribbler. First, whichever arm is controlling the ball needs to be relaxed at both the elbow and the wrist. Again, this will help prevent you from slapping at the ball. Your body should be low to the ground when you are dribbling. Not only will you move easier but you will also be able to better protect the ball from your defender.

Protect the Ball

As I just mentioned, protecting the ball is a crucial element of dribbling. If you are wild and careless with the ball, the other team will take it from you and you will

Proper dribbling position requires good knee flex, protecting the ball with your off hand, using your fingertips to control the ball, and keeping your head up so that you can see the court.

not have helped your team at all. A good way to stop this from happening is to keep the ball at waist level when you are bouncing it. If you let it come up too high, it will be difficult to control. And the whole point of dribbling is to maintain possession.

Keep Your Head Up

The end result of any good dribble is either a shot or a pass. If you can't see either the basket or your teammates because you are looking down at the ball or the floor, you won't be able to reach your goal. Practice enough so that your hands can maintain control of the ball while your eyes stay on what is going on around you. You have to be able to see your opponents to protect the ball. And you have to be able to see your teammates to know who is open to receive a pass. Later I'll present some drills that will help you get better at this.

The Sandlot

Pineland, Texas, the town where I grew up, is very small. It has a population of 862, two stores, one fire station, and no stop lights. It's so small you don't have to use the phone. All you have to do is yell out the door. There is not very much to do. But the one thing everybody *did* do was play basketball—on "the sandlot." The sandlot was nothing but a dirt court with two basketball hoops.

To get there, all I had to do was cross the street. I would get up early in the morning before school would start, run across the street at about 7 A.M., and make sure I had at least thirty or forty minutes of playing time before school. Mom never had to worry about waking me up to go to school. I was already up and on the court.

I was always playing ball. Always. From grammar school until senior year of high school, any time I saw someone playing ball, I was there. I was the only girl in Pineland that was so interested in basketball, and my dad didn't really want me out there with all those guys. He was afraid I was going to get hurt. But my mom would go against my dad and say, "Okay, Teresa, he's at work right now, you can go play. But make sure you get home before he gets here."

On weekends I would play ball all day. I wanted to play at night, too, but there weren't any lights in the sandlot, so the game would end when you couldn't see anymore.

The Speed Dribble

Now let's take a look at the speed dribble, which is used very often in the phase of the game called transition offense. When your team is on defense and gets possession of the ball by a rebound or a steal, you can sometimes start your offense so quickly that it catches the opposing team off-guard and you find yourself under your own basket with the defenders trailing behind. How did you get there? One way is with a quick dribble, where the ball is kept out in front of you while you are running behind it. You won't have to worry as much about protecting the ball because you are already clear of the defense, so shift your hand back on the ball to make it easier to push it farther ahead of you.

Advanced Dribbling

So you think you have control of the ball, and you want to take it to an advanced level. There are many fancy moves you can accomplish once you have possession of the ball on the dribble, and all of them can be effective weapons in a game. But remember, this is not about showing off. It is about making the best decision to help your team. However, if you can use a move off the dribble to shake loose from a defender and then shoot or deliver a pass, it is the right thing to do.

The Crossover

This is the point guard's favorite move and often her signature play. Simply put, it is about switching the ball from one hand to the other, thus leaving a defender facing the wrong direction. The reason for using the *crossover* is to change direction on the court. But unless it is done quickly and under control, the defender will take the ball and probably have a clear lane for a drive to her basket.

As you get near your defender, catch the outside of the ball on its way up in your primary dribbling hand. As you push your legs in that direction, force the ball the opposite way in front of you. Keep the ball low, to protect it, and as it heads toward your opposite hand, switch your weight in that direction as well. Then, as fast as you can,

The crossover dribble—an attacking move where the dribbler switches the ball from one hand to the other while maneuvering around the defender— must be executed quickly and under control. The quick change of direction often opens a clear lane to the basket.

start dribbling with that opposite hand and take it past your defender. If you can perfect a crossover dribble, you will always have an option for getting out of a tight defensive spot.

Hesitation (or the Fake)

The trick to this move is changing pace, altering the rate at which you are traveling, to confuse your defender, who you want to keep off-guard at all times. Imagine you are dribbling up the court and your defender is right there with you. Slow down and pull up your shoulders, making her think you are going to stop in one place. As she follows suit, you immediately accelerate with your speed dribble, and she is left behind.

The key here is to make an abrupt change; if your speed differential is only moderate, the defender will be able to adjust too easily. Another wrinkle you can throw in the hesitation move is a rocker step, which is a fake step to make your defender think you are headed one way when you are planning to go the other way. This is a good move to use if you have just received the ball from a teammate and are about to start your dribble. If, for example, you hold the ball above your head (to protect if from the defender) and rock your body with a step toward your left, the defender will think that's where you are headed. But in your mind you know you are going to use that momentum to go the other way and, hopefully, right by her.

Between the Legs and Behind the Back

Fans love these moves, but they are not the first ones you should be trying to learn. Add these to your game only after you have become accomplished with the control and speed dribbles. To perfect the dribble between your legs, stand with your legs apart and one in front of the other, like scissors. If your left leg is in the back, take the ball with your left hand in front of your body. Start dribbling, then

Dribbling between your legs is a move that requires a lot of practice to perfect. This move is intended for a quick change of direction without exposing the ball to the defender.

send it behind your right leg and through to your right hand. Catch the ball with your right hand and put it back in your other hand. Don't try to bounce it back through your legs, as this will never help you in a game. When you use this weapon, it will only be in one direction. Continue this motion to get used to it and then switch position, putting your left leg in front and starting the ball in front of you with your right hand.

The next step is to do it while you are moving. Start with your legs together while you are bouncing the ball. As you take a step forward, send the ball behind that leg. The ball should bounce at the same time as your step hits the ground. Stay low, with your hand closer to the ball, and try to bounce the ball through your legs with each step you take. With practice, you will be able to speed up and eventually use this in a game.

Dribbling behind your back is another effective way to rid yourself of a close defender. If the ball is in your right hand, take a step with your left leg and as you do, swing the ball behind you with the right hand, angling as much as you can toward your left hand, which you will be reaching behind you. As soon as your left hand catches it, head to your left with a speed dribble to get past your defender.

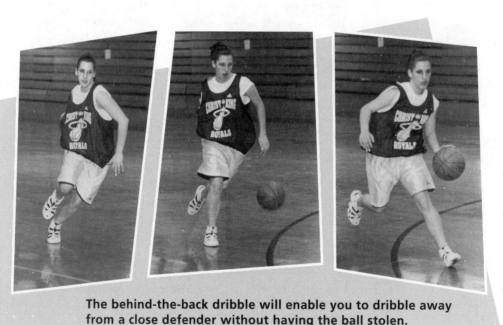

The behind-the-back dribble will enable you to dribble away from a close defender without having the ball stolen.

My Mom's Love

When I was growing up, my mom really placed my wings on properly. She taught me to fly. My mom always encouraged me to dream big and believe in myself. Always find a positive when negative things are coming. Even though I'm an adult now, I still turn to my mom when I need advice. When I need help or just want to feel good, all I have to do is to hear Mom's voice.

I know my mom has helped me become who I am today. She's always inspired me by making it through tough times, raising a family when we didn't have much, and later when she had a minor stroke and heart surgery. She never gave up. There may have been mountains, but she moved them to be where she is today. I've always said to her, "Mom, if I can be just half as strong as you are, I know I can be successful."

I know this is where my attitude comes from. My mother is a warrior, a true warrior, and that's the way I am when I play the game. I dedicate basically everything I do to my mother, because she made me who I am. That says a lot. I love you, Mom.

Use Both Hands

After learning about ways to dribble, I hope you have realized how important it is to be able to use both hands. Just like a successful soccer player uses both feet to advance the ball, you need to be able to rely on both hands to dribble. If you are right-handed, then you have to work twice as hard at using your left hand. If you are a lefty, practice twice as much with your right hand. If a defender realizes you can only go one way with the ball, she will have a much easier time defending you. Any drill you use to perfect your dominant hand, use it twice as much to perfect your weaker hand. Then, when a defender leaves the lane to her right wide open and you can dribble by her with your left hand, you will become a much more potent offensive weapon. Though it might feel strange to begin with, or you might feel so awkward that all you can do is bounce the ball off your foot, don't give up. The key to becoming a better player is to have the patience and confidence to make yourself stronger.

Driving to the Basket

Driving to the basket is an essential move for any player. The ability to "take it to the hole" will make defenders back off, creating space for you to take your jump shot.

So what is the end result of this babbling about dribbling? To score a basket. Obviously when you shake a defender loose you can pull up right away and take a jump shot. Or you can look for an open teammate who may be cutting to the basket or is already stationed underneath it, and she can score a layup. The third option is for you to continue dribbling all the way to the hoop and go straight up yourself for the shot. This is called *driving* to the basket, and any successful player needs to have this as an option. If you start your dribble near the foul line, also known as the top of the *key,* you can sometimes find an open lane right through the *paint* and up to the basket. Or if you dribble up the sideline, you can then drive along the baseline and come at the basket from the side. Here again using both hands is necessary. If you are right-handed and find yourself caught in the left corner of the court when the defender leaves the baseline open but you can't go around her to the left, you will have missed a chance to score. You don't want to go past her to the right, because other defenders will then be able to step in and stop you.

When I was young, I figured out my own way to improve my ball control for dribbling: I would dribble a tennis ball. If you can go up and down the floor dribbling a tennis ball the way you would a basketball, you're doing something really good. (Or as I sometimes say "You're handling your business.") Once you can control the tennis ball up and down the court, using both hands, you'll be amazed when you put the basketball in your hands. It's much easier to control the large basketball than the small tennis ball.

Dribbling Drills

Every player will be counted on at some point to handle the ball. Here are some drills that will help you become an accomplished dribbler.

Blindfold Drill

Cover your eyes with a mask and practice bouncing the ball. This will help your feel for the ball and improve your ability to keep your head up while dribbling.

Switching Hands

Run the length of the court dribbling with one hand and come back dribbling with the other. Then dribble up and down the court, changing hands with every bounce.

Obstacle Course

Set up cones, shoes, chairs, caps, T-shirts—whatever you can find—at equal distances from each other in a straight line down the court. Dribble around the cones like a driver on an obstacle course, switching hands as you go. As you get better, move the obstacles closer together.

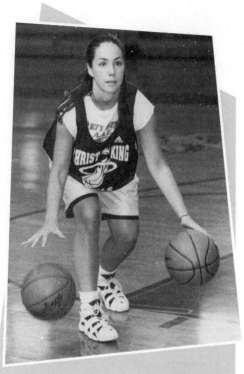

The two-ball dribbling drill will help you become a confident dribbler with either hand. Players who can dribble equally well with either hand are much harder to defend.

Two-Ball Drill

To help you with ball control and to help you dribble well with either hand, dribble with a ball in each hand. Try to walk the suicide drill (see page 9) while maintaining control of both basketballs.

Lying Down

It's easy to dribble standing up. Try this drill to keep your dribble going as your body changes position. Stand and dribble, then move down to your knees while still dribbling. Then sit on the floor, keeping the ball bouncing low and fast. Next lie down on your back while you continue to dribble. Try to dribble around your head to your other hand. Then reverse the process as you continue to bounce the ball, ending once again in a standing position.

Circle Drill

This one is for any number of players. Set yourselves up in a circle, each player dribbling a ball with one hand while trying to knock away anyone else's ball with the other hand. The object is to not lose your own ball. The last girl in the circle who still has a ball is the winner.

Around the Body

To get used to the feel of the ball, keep passing it from hand to hand around your head, then around your waist, then around your knees, and then your ankles, without dropping the ball. Go around each body part at least five times.

From Russia, with Love

In 1993 I was among the first Americans ever to play pro ball in Russia. And, boy, it sure was a challenge. We had come on the heels of an uneasy political relationship between the United States and Russia. No one spoke English on my team, and I didn't know Russian. We had to use sign language to communicate. I was there with fellow American Medina Dixon, and it took a while for our teammates to accept us. On top of the fact that we were Americans, we were taking some of their playing time away, so they would try to kill us in practice.

About two weeks into the season, Medina and I decided to play a trick on them to see if they really liked us. After a tough loss, we told them there was no need for us to be with them anymore. We weren't helping, so we would take the next flight home. Then the team got really quiet and a couple of girls who we thought hated us started crying. They said, "Don't leave." Then we finally told them it was a joke and realized that they had accepted us. After they got to know us, the team started to play with fire and to reel off wins. We grew to love it there in Russia and loved playing with those girls. I cherish the friendships I made with them because I had to earn their respect, love, and trust.

Now it's so interesting to go back to Russia and see how much the country has changed. Back then, you couldn't even take a picture of Red Square. Playing in Russia and Italy for nine years, I learned there's a lot to this world.

3

Passing

Passing is the most beautiful part of our game. Plus it's the most important skill in basketball. As a point guard, I know passing is also the most important part of my job. Unselfish teams, or passing teams, are usually good offensive teams. It's the quickest way to move the ball around the court. Passes create scoring opportunities. You only have a split second from the time you spot an open teammate before somebody guards her, and the only way to take advantage of that fleeting moment is with a crisp pass. A defense can never take a breather against a team that has a good passing game.

It's important to know the purpose of each pass. If you know what pass to make in a certain situation, you can eliminate potential turnovers. As a passer, you have the ability to make a teammate look great or terrible, depending on your pass. A good passer raises her teammates' level of play and confuses defenses. Passes are the most effective way to attack a defense. Plus an assist is just as important as a basket. Trust me on this one. I led the WNBA in assists last year, and our team went to the WNBA championship game.

Mother Knows Best

My mom remembers me as the little girl who would forget to come inside for meals because I was too busy playing basketball. "I always thought Teresa would be an outstanding person from the time she was small," my mom says. "She always loved children and old people. I taught her to do unto others as she would have them do unto her, and to this day I think she has. I tried to teach her to be herself, not to pattern herself after anybody."

Passing Fundamentals

- *Don't telegraph your passes.* This means, don't let your defender know who you are about to pass to by looking directly at your target the whole time you are preparing to pass the ball. So how do you avoid giving away your pass? Simply look away or fake the ball one way and then pass the other way. You can fake with your eyes by finding your teammate, then looking away from her. You can fake with your head by making believe you are about to shoot. The simplest way to create a *passing lane*—the lane through which you can pass the ball to a teammate—is by using a ball fake. You must understand how your opponent is playing defense and do a good acting job. For example, you can fake an overhead pass but throw a bounce pass. Practice looking one way to throw off the defense, then passing the other way. No-look passes might not work at first until you and your teammates become accustomed to one another's style of play. It may take some time before teammates aren't faked out by your fakes.

- *Pass away from the defense.* Direct your pass to a teammate on the side where the defender isn't.

- *Don't force the pass.* Check out the situation before passing. Let the defense make the first move, then respond.

- *Pass crisply.* A lazy pass can easily be intercepted.

- *Be careful when passing the ball across the court.* Throwing the ball across a sea of defenders is always risky.

Keep the pass out of the defender's reach. Always pass so that you lead your teammate to open space and away from the defender.

- *Hit the open player.* The open player is the player who is in the best position to score.

- *Know your teammates' abilities.* Can she catch a pass on the run and score? Does she have great hands? Knowing your teammates' preferences helps you make the right pass in the right situation. Remember, a pass is only good if it is caught. If you hit a player with a bullet right in her hands and she fumbles it, that doesn't do your team any good. As a passer you need to know what your teammates can handle.

- *Learn to pass with both hands.* If you're on the left side of the floor, pass with your left hand. If you're on the right side, pass with your right.

- *Communicate with your teammates.* Let your teammates know what to expect. It could be a signal with your hands, or eye contact, or a head fake—all nonverbal communication. For example, I don't even have to say a word to my Liberty teammate Vickie Johnson when we're on the court. We know each other's game so well, I can move my eyes a certain way and Vickie knows where I want her to go. And always remember to acknowledge a good pass. The assist means as much as the basket. That's what teamwork is all about.

My Dad, the Athlete

My dad, Charles, was an incredible athlete. He was a catcher and played minor-league baseball in the Minnesota Twins organization. He played in the early sixties in the South— a time that was difficult for blacks. He always questions what his career would have been like if he had played at a later time in history and made it to the majors. Still, he doesn't regret in any way what he went through. He enjoyed playing and loved the experience even though times were tough. In fact, it was these tough times that made him a stronger man.

Types of Passes

There are many different ways to pass the ball. Each method is effective when executed properly and at the right time. It's just as important to know when and how to pass as it is to know when and how to shoot.

The Chest Pass

The chest pass is used more than any other pass in the game. It is effective because the ball is thrown with the force of two hands. Hold the ball with both hands at chest level. Your hands should be up, your fingers spread, and your thumbs pointed toward each other. Keep your elbows in and bent. Take a step toward the teammate you are passing to and push your hands away from your chest. As you release the ball, shift your weight from your back foot to your front foot and follow through. Your arms should be fully extended, and your thumbs should rotate toward the floor. Don't float your pass. Follow through to your target, and get your weight behind the pass. A short chest pass gets the ball to your teammate as quickly as possible.

To make a crisp, accurate chest pass, bring the ball in toward your chest with two hands. Step at the target with your lead foot and push the ball to your teammate, snapping your wrists to increase velocity. Your hands should point outward on the follow-through.

The Bounce Pass

The bounce pass is often used on the fast break. It's a must when a defender has her hands over her head or when you have to slip the ball by a taller defender (because the defender will have trouble getting down to deflect it). It also is handy when you're in a tight spot, surrounded by waving arms, in a situation too risky to throw a chest pass. It is difficult to intercept because a defender must reach down to the floor to get a hand on the ball. Also, the pass is softer to receive, so a bounce pass helps a teammate get a head start on the play. Hold the ball just as you do when making a chest pass. Your thumbs should face inward when you release the ball. Step toward your teammate as you throw. The ball should bounce on the floor about two-thirds of the way to your teammate so that it can be caught at waist level. If the ball is any higher, it will be an easy steal for the defense. Also, if the ball bounces too close to your teammate, it will reach her near her calf and will be too tough to handle.

To practice your bounce pass, position a teammate about twelve feet away. Aim for a spot on the floor two-thirds of the way to your teammate. Make sure you use both hands and step toward the target.

The Overhead Pass

The overhead pass is used to make an outlet pass to begin a fast break, to swing the ball from one side of the court to the other, or off a rebound in traffic. Throwing with two hands over your head gives your pass distance, speed, and accuracy. The ball should be held just above your head, with your hands and your fingers spread on each side. (Do not put the ball behind your head, because it can be easily stolen.) Support the ball with your fingertips. Your elbows should be bent and your wrists cocked. Your feet should be staggered so that your weight shifts from your back foot to your front foot as you move the ball from the top of your head forward. Release the ball in front of your head. Your fingers and wrists should snap forward toward your target. Follow through with your arms extended—like a chest pass, only higher.

Players often use the overhead pass when the defender has them trapped in a corner. It's especially useful for taller players.

The baseball pass is used to throw the ball a long distance. Fast breaks and outlets downcourt commonly require players to use the baseball pass.

The Baseball Pass

The baseball pass, just as the name says, is thrown like a baseball. This one-handed pass allows you to throw the ball a long distance. Stagger your feet and support the ball primarily in one hand. Shift your weight backward and guide the ball from just behind the shoulder of your throwing side. When throwing, your passing hand extends forward. The ball is released as your arm straightens. Step into your pass, and put an arc on the ball so it will go farther and be easier to catch.

The Behind-the-Back Pass

The behind-the-back pass is a crowd pleaser that is difficult to master. It's done on the move and can catch the defense by surprise. With the ball in the palm of your passing hand, take the ball behind your back and flip it, snapping your wrist and following through in the direction of your target.

In order to execute each of these passes, you've got to practice them repeatedly. Some good passers—like Larry Bird—are born; the rest of us have to work hard at it.

Passing Drills

Rapid-Fire Drill

You can practice your passing by yourself if you use a wall. This drill will help you develop the chest pass, the overhead pass, and the baseball pass. It will help you learn to catch hard passes, deliver the ball quickly, strengthen your hands and wrists, and develop your hand-eye coordination.

Stand about two feet from the wall. Make a hard chest pass against it. As you make each quick pass, back up until you are standing ten feet away from the wall. Repeat this drill with the overhead pass and the baseball pass. On the baseball pass, practice throwing with each hand.

Line Drill

If you are practicing with a group, break up into two lines. Players at the front of the line face each other, about fifteen feet apart. Player 1 chest-passes the ball to Player 2. Then Player 1 moves to the end of Player 2's line. Player 2 passes the ball to Player 3 and then moves to the end of Players 1 and 3's line. When Player 1 and Player 2 return to the front of their respective lines, try a bounce pass, then an overhead pass, and a baseball pass.

Monkey in the Middle

This is a three-person drill that helps create pressure with the defense. You can work on bounce passes or overhead passes. Stand about fifteen feet across from the other player with the third player (the defender) in the middle. You have the ball, and the defender hustles over to contest the pass. When the ball is thrown, the player in the middle sprints to cover the new passer. Do not pass the ball until the defense has arrived. The defender stays in the middle and defends both passers until she gets a deflection or until five passes are thrown. Switch positions and repeat the drill.

Good players can execute a pass at any time. A relaxed appearance may catch the defender off-guard, allowing the ball to be delivered quickly and accurately.

No-Dribble Scrimmage

Try to play a game in which none of the players are allowed to dribble. This helps players look for the open teammate and learn how to get open. You'll see how a team can really work together through passing.

Passing on the Run

Line up opposite a teammate, about six feet apart. Make crisp chest passes back and forth as you run straight ahead for thirty yards. Hold the follow-through until your pass is caught. Make sure you keep a constant distance between each other, and then return to the starting point. Repeat with bounce passes. This helps improve your passing and catching while on the run.

Two at Once

Stand about eight feet from a teammate. Each person has a ball. One of you is the bounce passer, the other is the chest passer. Make your passes, to each other at the same time and make them fast. Make fifty passes, then switch roles. Be sure to follow through and watch the ball as it comes into your hands.

School First, Basketball Second

My dad was really strict. He always stressed education, something that has stayed with me. He told us, "Do your homework first and then go out and play." He always asked me, "Where's your books?" I did my homework at school—at recess—so I could play after school. If my dad hadn't been that way, if he wasn't that strong and stern with us, where would we be? Even though I've received many athletic accolades, my greatest accomplishment in high school was being valedictorian of my class.

4

Shooting and Individual Offense

We all know the first way to get yourself noticed on the basketball court is to make shots. Start hitting from the outside, and fans in the stands will wonder, "Who is that girl?"

June, Dinky, K.K., Mike, and NeeCee

I idolized my oldest brother, Charles Jr. (June), as a kid. He was good at any sport he played. But Charles has experienced a lot of pain in his life. The reason he isn't playing pro sports today (he played football and baseball for Prairie View A&M and had a pro tryout with the Dallas Cowboys) is because in his younger years he became addicted to drugs and lost out on basically everything. He always tells me to this day to please share his story because kids will hear it and learn from it. The amazing thing about Charles is that he was honest and strong enough to admit he had a problem. Charles got help and is now fully recovered. He's been off drugs for eleven years and has a great job. I'm so very proud of him.

My oldest sister, Diana (Dinky), taught me to be strong. She sacrificed her natural athletic ability to help out the five other kids in the family, especially me. She was a shining light in our family; she helped us grow up and helped my mother when my parents separated. She's only about five-feet-four, but in high school she won the state long jump championship. She gave up all of that in order to help the rest of us.

A great thing about my sister, Carolyn (K.K.), is that she

taught me how to be very neat and how to be a lady. Now she's the one we call stingy; the girl knows how to save money. She taught me how to better myself financially. She's truly a strong point in our family, and she's my number one cheerleader.

My mom always says that my brother Michael (Mike) and I should have been twins. If he feels something, I can feel it, too. It's amazing. He gets more excited about me than I do about myself. It excites him more than anything in the world that his little sister is finally doing what she wants to do, playing pro basketball in the United States. Mike taught me to always stay calm, to stay focused. He has been with me from step one to two to three to four. He always will be. He's my heart.

Denise (NeeCee) is the sibling closest to me in age. She had a huge health problem, and we almost lost her on my twenty-seventh birthday. She has taught all of us how to survive.

Shooting the Rock

It takes a lot of work to become a good shooter. Practice, form, patience—all of these things go into good shooting. But remember, being able to make a shot consistently is not enough to make you a good player. Shooting is one phase of the game, and when you can combine it with solid ballhandling, crisp passing, tenacious defense, and a good attitude, you will be well on your way to becoming a fine player. Close attention to proper form is the only sure way of knocking down your shots on a regular basis. Your fingers, hands, eyes, and legs must all work together to ensure success.

Hand Position

Proper hand position on the ball is the first step in finding the bottom of the net.

Place your dominant hand at an angle underneath the basketball, centered with your fingers spread wide. If you need a guide, find the valve hole used for inflating the basketball and place your middle finger on this spot. Your palm, as in dribbling, should not be flush against the ball. Leave a sliver of air and control the ball with your fingers. Your arm should then be in an L position underneath the ball, in line with the basket. Do not let it angle outward when you shoot, or your aim will be off. Your other hand is used to guide the ball while your domi-

Representing

After my first season with the Liberty, the one thing I knew I really wanted to improve was my shot. I won the league's Defensive Player of the Year, but I didn't want opponents to be able to lay off of me on offense. So I spent the winter playing with guys here in New York. They taught me a lot about New York–style basketball, which is not about being fancy but about showing off the beauty of the game, being entertaining. I did most of my workouts at the Reebok Club in Manhattan, where a lot of guys would come in to play me. I told them, "If you're going to play me like I'm a girl, I don't want to play. See me like an athlete right now. When I walk away, then you can see me as a girl." This made them play even tougher. At times they'd knock me down so hard it seemed like they were trying to kill me. And if they asked me if I was okay, I'd really get angry. I would tell them, "Wait till you go down the next time, I'm not going to ask you if you're okay."

nant hand shoots it. The weak hand should be lined up on the side of the ball but should be used only to guide it, not to shoot it. If you apply too much pressure from the side, the ball will not spin correctly and your shot will be off-line.

Using Your Legs

Shooting may look like it all comes from your arms, but it doesn't. The strength to get the ball to the basket comes just as much from your legs. Begin by balancing your weight, distributing it evenly to the balls of both feet. Bend your knees and stagger your feet about shoulder width apart. The foot on the side of your shooting hand should be a little bit ahead of your other foot. Now that you are balanced, make sure to keep your body straight and your shoulders square to the basket (with both shoulders an equal distance from the hoop) when you shoot. Do not lean forward, as this will make your shot too hard or might cause you to bang into a defender and be whistled for an offensive foul. And don't fall back, as you will lose strength on the shot. Bend your knees and release the ball as you spring upward. This gives you added power, which you will not get if you shoot with your arms only. Using your whole body also gives you better accuracy.

Your legs are the foundation of your shot. Make sure your feet are under you and squared to the basket. If you don't think legs are important to your shot, try hitting a three-pointer from your knees.

Release and Follow-through

Now you are ready to let the ball go from your fingertips with the strength of your body behind it. As it leaves your hands, it is important that the ball has the proper spin, which is backspin. Anything else is wrong. How does it get backspin? It's the combination of your hands being placed properly and your body following through. As you raise the ball to shoot, don't release when it is in front of your face, thus blocking your view of the basket. It should be nearer to your forehead, so that your arms will create an open space—a window—for you to look through.

When you shoot, spring your body and snap your wrist as you let go. Aim for a high arc on the shot, not a line drive toward the rim. A hard shot will not be as forgiving as it reaches the basket; if it is at all off-line, it will bounce away hard. A softer touch and a higher arc give the ball more room to fall into the basket and more opportunity for bounces off the rim to go through the net. Proper backspin as a result of a strong wrist snap will also help provide the soft touch.

After you have let go of the ball with primary pressure coming from your middle three fingers, continue the movement of your hand so that

The ball is actually released from the fingertips and above the shooter's face.

To become a great shooter, you must follow through. Following through provides backspin on the ball, creating a softer touch that allows more shots to fall through the hoop.

your wrist bends all the way forward and your fingers end up pointing to the ground. (Some people say it makes your arm look like a goose, but I like to think it looks more like a swan.) Good follow-through might seem like an afterthought, but it truly helps the flight of the ball after it has left your hand.

One other important factor is to keep your eyes on the basket, not on the ball or your defender. Focus on the rim and aim for that. Or, if you plan to use the backboard, focus on the box painted on it.

Three Basic Shots

Now that your form is fine, what kind of shot are you going to take? There are plenty of varieties. Different game situations require different shots. The best players master as many shot types as they can.

The Layup

This is perhaps the easiest shot in basketball but also the most important. The majority of points scored in a game are from layups. A layup

Drive hard to the basket and finish softly when executing a layup.

is a basket scored very close to the hoop and usually is the end result of a drive to the basket. You want to begin by learning the proper way to shoot the layup from a standing position, and once you have mastered that, you should start adding the dribble before it so you can use it to drive to the hole during a game.

Pick the side of the basket where you are going to take your first layup. Start with your dominant hand (that is, from the right if you are right-handed). Later, switch to the opposite side, as it is very important to practice layups with both hands and from both sides of the basket. Holding the ball with the proper hand placement, plant your weakside foot (if you are shooting with your right hand, plant your left foot). Then lift your right knee as you leap vertically. Release the ball while your body is on the way up. This, too, may seem like an awkward motion, but the more you do it, the better you will become.

As you feel more comfortable with the layup motion, move back a step, dribble the ball once as you step with your right foot, plant the left foot on the next step, and take the layup. With each level of comfort, add more dribbles, always ending with a firmly planted foot. Then start the whole process by leading with your weak hand so you can be good at using either hand.

Here are some other important things to remember about taking layups:

- *Aim high on the backboard.* This improves the chances of the ball going in.

- *Don't shoot too close to the basket.* This diminishes your angle at the rim. Leave room to move freely.

- *Go up straight.* Leaning into the defender makes it easier for her to guard you and draw an offensive foul.

- *Keep your eyes on the backboard and the hoop, not on the ball.* Your target is the hoop or the backboard, and that's where your eyes should be focused.

- *Don't be afraid to be strong.* Though you don't want to deliberately knock someone over, because you will be committing a foul, you do need to be aggressive. The layup will rarely be uncontested in a game, so go in strong. Even if you feel you've been fouled, finish the play. If the foul is called, you will be awarded a free throw and a chance to complete a three-point play.

Later, you can add the *reverse layup* to your arsenal. This is when you dribble up one side of the lane, then switch sides by dribbling so you can take the layup from the opposite side. This shot works best when the ball rolls off the tips of your fingers. It is a wonderful weapon to avoid a defender who could block your shot. Make the switch before you plant your foot, and dribble to the other side. Then take the shot with the same hand you would have used before you switched sides. That is, if you dribbled up the right, then moved to your left, you would still take the shot with your right hand leading.

Players who compete at an advanced level can add the finger roll to their arsenal of offensive weapons.

West Sabine High School, in Pineland, was a small school, so we played other small schools. But our coach, Retha Swindell, started to schedule games with the bigger schools in Texas so we'd get some fiercer competition. When we beat the bigger schools, that taught us we could play with anybody. If you put your mind to it and work hard, you can play with anybody. That's the way I feel. We didn't win any championships, but we always came close.

Jump Shot

The jump shot has become the most popular weapon in basketball; any girl who can hit the jumper with consistency has a chance to be a real player. The jump shot is taken after you pick up your dribble, which gives you momentum or puts you into proper position to have an open look at the basket. As soon as you pick up your dribble, square yourself to the basket and jump as you shoot. Releasing the ball when you are in the air makes it more difficult for your opponent to

These two photos illustrate the difference between the set shot and the jump shot. For the set shot, the ball is released while the toes are still touching the ground. The shooter releases the ball at the peak of her jump when shooting a jump shot.

defend the shot. Here, as with any shot, the strength of your legs can help tremendously. The higher you are able to jump, the farther away from a defender you can get. As with the layup, make sure your jump is vertical, so that your aim will be its straightest and the shot won't drift to the left or right. And don't forget to follow through, which is necessary to make it a good shot.

Hook Shot

What makes the hook shot different from the others we have learned about so far is that it is taken with only one hand. The hook shot should be reserved for times when you are near the basket, as it doesn't have enough strength behind it to travel far. It is taken by shooting the ball over the top of your head from behind, so that it hooks over your head. Obviously, you will not be able to square up to the basket like you would on a jump shot, but what the hook

The hook shot is a great tool for players who set up down in the low post. Once it's practiced and executed correctly, it becomes nearly impossible to defend.

shot does is catch your opponent by surprise. The hook shot is very difficult to defend because you start it with your back to the basket and, thus, to your defender. If you are shooting with your right hand, pivot around to your left on the ball of your left foot. Your body will be at a right angle to the basket. Bring the ball up your right side, then swing it in a high arc over your head, releasing the ball at the top of the arc. As with any good shot, the ball should come off your fingertips and have backspin.

Three-Point Shot

Once you feel confident taking all three basic shots, you should work on increasing your range. That is, being able to shoot farther away from the basket. The three-point shot is a great weapon in basketball, and if you can hit from way downtown, you will be a more complete player. The key is practice and repetition. Once you can hit shots consistently from one spot on the floor, take a few steps back and start again. Don't begin your practice by taking shots from three-point range; they are difficult, and repeated misses can be discouraging. Start close to the basket and work your way out.

The key to becoming a good shooter is taking good shots. Quality shots are created through the hard work of each offensive player on the floor.

Shot Selection

What makes a good shot? Obviously one that goes in. But let's be more specific. A good shot is the right shot at the right time. Should the center be taking jump shots from fifteen feet out? Probably not. The role of a post player is to stay in the paint area, moving in and out to receive passes from the guards and to make layups. But if a guard takes that jumper and her range is consistently good enough, that is a good shot. To become a smart player rather than one who just has good skills, you need to be thinking all the time on the court. If the other team has just scored ten straight points, do you want to come right down and pull up for a jumper? No. You want to slow things down and help your team get its offensive rhythm back. If you are not sure what a good shot is in a particular situation, ask your coach when you are at practice.

Free Throws

The free throw is the only uncontested shot in a basketball game. A player is awarded free throws when she is fouled while attempting a shot. If the shot does not go in, the player gets two foul shots (or three on a missed three-pointer). If the shot goes in, she is awarded one free throw. Foul shots very often make the difference in determining which team wins a basketball game. If you score five more field goals than your opponent but miss ten or fifteen more free throws, you will lose even if it seems that you outplayed your opponent. And nothing is more frustrating than missing foul shots, which should be a given. Where teams that shoot 50 percent from field goal range are considered very successful, the best players and teams should be able to hit 70 percent to 80 percent of their free throws.

   You take a free throw from the foul line, while teammates and opponents line up to await the rebound. Use the same form discussed earlier: bending your knees, squaring your shoulders, eyeing the basket, and following through. Make sure you are comfortable before taking the shot (you are allowed to take some dribbles first) but don't wait too long because you

Success from the free-throw line is a product of focus, confidence, and hours of practice.

only have ten seconds to take the shot. If it is late in the game and it will help to catch a few deep breaths, this is a good time to do so. A smart idea is to practice free throws when you are tired, such as at the end of practice or after you have been running. This will best simulate a game situation. Free throws are often the difference late in the game, when the score is close and the teams are trading trips to the foul line. The clock is stopped with each free-throw trip, so often players will foul deliberately if they need the time to catch up in the score. But if it is your team that is ahead and you can make the free throws, you will win.

Triple Threat

How do you approach your decision of what to do with the ball once you have received it from a teammate via a pass? The answer is the triple-threat position. Start by squaring up and facing the basket. This puts you in the triple threat, which means you are now ready to

Lesson Learned

Once during my senior year at Louisiana Tech, Coach Barmore told me before a game against Pepperdine that I wasn't starting. He said I hadn't begun the season the way he wanted me to. I was mad, of course. I thought I was playing hard. After calming down, I realized that he was trying to teach me that I could be an All-American, I could win a national championship, and I could be the playmaker of the 1988 Olympic team, but that I had to work even harder in my last year in school. That's when I started to play with more aggression. He taught me that what I had inside of me hadn't truly exploded yet. I had even more in me than I knew.

shoot, pass, or dribble. When the girl guarding you sees you are ready to do any of these three things, it is harder for her to defend you. By positioning your hands correctly and holding the ball safely near your waist, you have the element of surprise on your side and the ability to carry it out.

Drill That Shot

Shooting a basketball is like most other activities—practice makes perfect. However, practice doesn't pay off if it isn't done correctly. Use the drills described below and your shooting touch should improve quickly.

Layup Drills

Give yourself a thirty-second time limit and start taking layups from one side. Catch your own rebound and see how many baskets you can successfully score in the time limit. Do the same thing from the other side of the hoop. This will improve your touch and speed.

The triple-threat position allows the ball handler to shoot, pass, or dribble.

Around the World

This is a great driveway game, in which you set up spots around the semicircular key and take shots from each spot. Start directly in front of the basket, then at one baseline, then at the corner next to the free-throw line, then at the free-throw line, then at the other corner, the other baseline, and back to the middle. Then reverse the order. The object is to be the first player to make all the shots around the world and back again. The rules are simple. If you make the shot, you move to the next spot, until you miss. Then it's the next player's turn. You do have the option, however, of taking a chance, which means risking another shot. If you miss that, you go back a spot on your next turn. If you make it, your turn continues.

Twenty-one

In this game, you start with a shot from behind the free-throw line. If you make it, it is worth three points. Then you grab your own rebound and take a jumper from that spot. A made shot is worth two points. Then grab the rebound, drive, and take a layup, which is worth one point. Each turn has a maximum potential of six points. The first to twenty-one points wins. But here's the catch—you have to score *exactly* twenty-one points, so you better brush up on your math as well.

Horse

This is a really fun game where you can be creative. It starts with one player making a shot. When she makes it, all the other players have to duplicate the exact same shot. If they miss, they are saddled with an *H,* the first letter in *horse.* After everyone tries, the next player attempts to set a new standard. But each miss earns another letter, and you are out of the game when you get *H-O-R-S-E.* The final girl remaining is the winner.

Layup Line

This is a good team drill. You divide into two equal groups and start at midcourt on either side of the foul line. Every player in one line has a ball. The first player in that line dribbles up the court and takes a layup. She is trailed by the first player from the opposite line, who grabs the rebound and takes the ball with her to the end of the layup line. The girl who just took the layup heads to the end of the rebound line, and the lines continue to flow. This can also work with jump shots.

Keep a Running Count

Repetition is the best form of practice, so if you want to be a really good shooter, try to take between three hundred and five hundred shots at practice in addition to one hundred free throws. Keep track of how many you make, and you will be pleasantly surprised at your improvement over a short period of time.

Practice your form, too. Though you won't always have a basket nearby, that shouldn't stop you. Even if you are sitting in your living room, you can release a basketball just above your head and catch it again. This repetition of shooting form, with your hands properly positioned and your fingers and wrist following through, will make it natural.

Gimme the Ball!

When I was in college and the game came down to the final shot, I always wanted to be the one to shoot the ball. I didn't want somebody else to be in that situation and not be able to handle it if the ball didn't go in the hole. Once I lost a game against Northeast Louisiana at the free-throw line and felt terrible.

But you can't let that kind of thing get you down, because what are you going to do the next time you get in that very same situation? Are you going to get there and start shaking because you missed it the last time? Or are you going to get up there and say, "This time I won't miss it"? You have to tell yourself, "I will not miss it. I will not let my teammates down."

When you miss a shot and the other team is celebrating, you look at your teammates and you tell them, "I guarantee you it won't happen again." That's the first thing I felt when it happened to me. I'm going to hurt, but I'm not going to beat myself over it. And when I get back on the court, it's done. It's over. I can't do anything about it. I can't change it. The only time I can redeem myself is when I get back in that position. And it's going to go in. It's falling.

Above all, be creative with your shooting drills. Pretend you are in a game situation. Put pressure on yourself to make a clutch shot. Time how many shots you can take in a certain number of seconds. Get friends to play with you, and have fun. Any player who has reached the professional ranks is full of stories about how much time she spent shooting—in gyms, on playgrounds, or in driveways.

5

Rebounding

Dennis Rodman, who plays for the Chicago Bulls, is one of the greatest rebounders of all time because he has a nose for the ball after a missed shot. Rebounding is truly one of the dirtiest jobs in the game but one of the most rewarding. Whichever team wins the battle of the boards usually controls the game. If you allow a team to get second or third shots, your team will have a tough time winning.

There are two kinds of rebounds, defensive and offensive. Defensive rebounds result when your team recovers your opponent's missed basket. The better job you do with defensive rebounds, the fewer chances your opponent will have to score. Offensive rebounding is when you recover your own team's missed shot. The better job you do on that end, the more shots your team will have. And remember, you don't have to be six feet tall to be a great rebounder. Even though I'm not the tallest person on the court, I can still hold my own. And I love the feeling of pulling down a rebound with power and authority.

Celebrity Row

Playing for the Liberty, I met people I never dreamed of meeting. I talked to President Clinton on the phone after the championship game; I've become good pals with supermodel Tyra Banks, who is now my occasional workout partner; I joked with Rosie O'Donnell on the court and on her show; I made a guest appearance on an episode of Bill Cosby's sitcom, The Cosby Show; I even dunked McNuggets with Grant Hill for a McDonald's commercial.

Because I don't have a shy bone in my body, sometimes I would shimmy along the sideline in front of dancer/actor Gregory Hines. Other times I would high-five his entire row. I don't know what comes over me. I guess what makes me so comfortable doing that is that I'm in my territory, on the court. They're in my place; they're in my home.

During breaks in games, I sometimes chat up the folks in the front rows at Madison Square Garden, big celebrities and small kids alike. Because everyone took time out of their schedules to be a part of what we are trying to do, which is to touch the lives of other people, I think it is my duty to thank them for being there.

The Rules of Rebounding

Always assume every shot is a miss. Don't watch the flight of the ball. Move into prime rebounding position where you think the ball will come off the rim or backboard. The best position is three to four feet away from the basket. Timing is critical in rebounding; jump a second too early or a second too late and you'll likely never get the ball. Stay on the balls of your feet, ready to move and react. You must be ready to jump at the ball like a tiger. Be aggressive. Grab the ball like you mean it. But be careful not to foul—to climb over a player's back (to go "over the top"). Instead, go up straight for the ball. Jump up, not forward. Keep your hands up and elbows out, hogging up as much space as possible.

Grabbing rebounds is a combination of anticipation, positioning, and boxing out your opponent. Guards should keep this in mind even if they're standing out near the top of the key.

Anticipate

A good rebounder anticipates where a shot will land. Consider that the ball rebounds to the opposite of the basket most times. So if a shot is taken to the left of the lane, it likely will rebound to the right. If the shot is a long-range jumper, the rebound should be longer. Bank shots usually rebound closer to the basket. Read a shot to see if it's going to fall short or long, and anticipate where the rebound might go. Look for the quickest route to the ball. The key is quickness. Once you have the rebound, don't panic with the ball. Pivot away from your opponents and try to make an outlet pass.

Want It

Rebounding is mostly about desire. You have to want the ball. Great rebounders think every missed shot is their ball and they go for the ball every time a shot is taken. Don't worry about going up against a bigger player, because if you want the ball more than she does, you'll get it.

Box Out

You want to establish a position between your opponent and the basket when the shot is in the air. Rebounding is the most physical part of basketball. Find the player you are guarding, make contact with your opponent (your rear end to her knees), and maintain it. When you lose your player, her job becomes much easier. You must get low (the lower you are, the better) and have good balance when boxing out. Resist the temptation to go up for a ball and to forget your opponent on a rebound. Once you have the inside position and you have boxed out your girl, go for the rebound. Jump for the ball with both feet for the most power. If no one is around you, you can jump faster and higher with one foot. Remember, rebounding is an entire team's responsibility. If four people work hard and box out properly and the fifth player doesn't, that won't do the team much good because it could be her player who gets the ball.

Face the basket and make contact with your opponent (your rear end to her knees). If you feel your opponent trying to get around you, shuffle with her, maintaining contact at all times. Once you see the ball come off the basket, leap straight up toward the ball with two hands. Grab the rebound and protect the ball.

Protect the Ball

Always use two hands to get the ball, because there will be a swarm of defenders around ready to strip it from you. If you can't grab it with both hands, tip it to a teammate. Once you have the ball, protect it like a prized possession. Bring it down with both arms to your chest. And to keep the ball away from your opponent, use your body as a shield and pivot. Use your elbows, knees, and body to protect the ball and keep it high. Don't bring the ball down for opponents to steal. Be careful not to swing your elbows. And don't put the ball down to dribble around all those players under the basket, because it's too dangerous. You'll be asking to get it stolen.

After a defensive rebound, you want to react quickly and go from defense to offense by pushing the ball downcourt yourself or getting it downcourt with an outlet pass to a teammate down the sidelines. If there is no one open, bring the ball down to your chest and hold it until the frenzy under the basket clears. Then dribble up the court or pass it to a teammate.

Offensive Rebounding

Defensive rebounding is hard work, but offensive rebounding is even tougher. Why? Because usually you're farther from the basket and have to get around your opponent to get the inside position.

Rule No. 1: Always follow your shot. The moment your shot leaves your hand, get ready to rebound it. As the shooter, you will be able to feel whether the shot is long or short and where to position yourself. If you rebound the ball, put it right back up without hesitation. And if you can't get the ball, tip it to a teammate.

Rule No. 2: Anticipate when your teammate is going to release a shot. If you do get boxed out, try to get around your player. Cut or fake one way, then go the other. Don't get caught watching your shot or a shot by one of your teammates. Move immediately. Go for every rebound. Be aggressive.

An advanced player looks to throw an outlet pass as she is coming down with the rebound.

Rebounding Drills

Now let's go over some rebounding drills that will help you be more like Dennis Rodman (and I'm not talking about his hair color). Remember, your team can't score unless you get the ball. Hit the boards hard!

Line Drill

Line up one behind the other. The first player in line banks the ball off the backboard, and the next person in line jumps to get the ball and throws it against the backboard. And so on. After each turn, players go to the end of the line.

It's wonderful to be a positive role model for kids, but it's extraspecial to be a positive influence on the lives of Anthony, Tanaya, Dominique, Brandon, and Jalen, my nieces and nephews. They help me continue to stay focused on using my ability to inspire others. I want them, and all kids, to know that all things are possible.

Superkid Drill

Stand on the block outside the foul lane. Face the basket. Toss the ball over the rim to the opposite side of the backboard using a chest pass. Throw it high and then go retrieve the ball. Catch the ball on the other side, then start again, throwing the ball over the rim to the opposite side. Do this drill for thirty seconds. Rest between each set, or shoot foul shots. Then repeat two more times.

Power Drill

Face the basket. Start in front of the backboard on the right side with the ball in both hands over your head. Jump five times with the ball in this position. On your last jump, pull the ball down and make a ball fake. Then go up for a power move to the basket and shoot. Do the same on the left side. Complete two sets of ten on each side. Rest between each set, or shoot foul shots.

Tip Drill

Start at the foul line. Toss the ball underhanded off the right side of the backboard with your right hand. Tip the ball with one hand to an open space on the same side. Then grab the rebound and sprint back to the foul line. Do the same for the left side. Tip five times on each side and repeat three times. Rest between sets.

Offensive Rebounding Drill

Start at the foul line and throw the ball underhanded to the left side of the backboard using your left hand. Explode to the ball and grab the rebound with both hands. Fake, then make a layup. Alternate sides. Make five layups from both sides. Repeat three times. Rest between sets.

Box Out Drill

Pair up with teammates and jog around the court together. Both players in each pair try to gain the inside position. However, the players are not allowed to have contact until your coach calls, "Shot!" Then everyone boxes out.

My Hoops Heroes

When I was young and watching the NBA, there were so many point guards that I had so much respect for and wanted to be like. The heart of Isiah Thomas was amazing. He played so hard. Michael Jordan is a gifted athlete, but he also tears people up mentally. I loved watching Magic Johnson—he was show time, and a true leader. When you're allowed to lead, it's amazing the level you can bring another player to. Magic was incredible at that. I had the opportunity to meet him during an NBA All-Star weekend and he said to me, "Spoon, it's about bringing your team to another level. Leaders are vocal and you have that. Bring them to another level so they have an opportunity to feel what it's like." And then he called me show time. I still can't believe it.

6

Individual Defense

It is a common plea from coaches in all sports: Offense gets the headlines, but defense wins the games. Playing tough defense is certainly not glamorous. Only the trained basketball fan will notice a player who is working the hardest on defense. Casual fans will always notice the scorers and offensive stars first. But that's no reason to relax when the other team has the ball. Playing good defense comes from having pride in what you do, having more desire than the next person on the roster. Desire is the root of good defense. When Michael Jordan was described as a great offensive player who wasn't a great defender, he took it as a personal challenge. Now he is one of the league's best defenders and consistently makes the all-NBA defensive team. That's desire to prove to yourself that you can try hard and be dedicated to achieving a goal.

Part of that desire is shown in how aggressively you play defense. It's not enough just to react to what the other player does; you must also be thinking all the time about what you can do to rattle your opponent. Going for steals, diving for a loose ball, denying your opponent the ball, altering the direction she is trying to dribble—all of these things will rattle her and make you a more effective defender.

Jesse Owens

One athlete I really look up to is Jesse Owens. He was one of the first to open up track and field for African Americans during a time when Adolf Hitler was spreading the myth of white supremacy. During the Berlin Olympics, in 1936, Owens needed only 10.3 seconds to shatter Hitler's thinking. He raced to the gold in the hundred-meter dash. He also won the gold in three other events. Without Jesse Owens there would be no Carl Lewis, no Jackie Joyner-Kersee, no Michael Johnson. He has challenged us all. Let's meet the challenge.

Positioning and Footwork

If you want to play good defense, the first thing to do is to get yourself in the proper position. Like shooting or dribbling, the way your body is set up can make a world of difference in your game. It may seem like too many positions to remember—where your legs should be, how your hands should be placed. But the more you play, the more natural these stances will become. The more natural they become, the more easily you will be able to switch from one phase of the game to another during the course of a real contest. The more games you play, the more you won't even realize you have just switched, because your body will react the right way without thinking.

Shuffle

So what's the correct way to position yourself for defense? Like many other phases of the game, it begins with balance. You need to be ready to move at all times, because you have to follow your opponent and sometimes the ball. The defensive stance should see you with your knees bent and your weight on the balls of your feet. Resting back on your heels will make you slower, making it easier for your opponent to dribble by you if she has the ball or to get open for a pass if she doesn't. One foot should be slightly in front of the other, and your feet should be about shoulder width apart. The best way to move on defense is with a *shuffle step*. This is where your feet move from side to side, rather than crossing over each other. Later we will go over a shuffle drill to help you get better at this.

Keep your knees bent and arms out when defending the ball handler. Stay on the balls of your feet so you can quickly shuffle to the left or right.

Imagine you are guarding your opponent, and she is dribbling to her left to try to get around you. Your right foot (which will be nearest to the ball) should step toward the right, with the left foot following so that you are back in your defensive stance but a full step over to the right. If you cross your feet, you will slow yourself down, you might get your legs tangled, and your opponent will be able to switch directions quickly, leaving you behind. That is a no-no on defense. You have to do your best to stay with her at all times. The only time you should end up crossing your feet and running the regular way is if you have allowed your opponent to get by you and you need to catch up. Once you have done that, return to the ready stance and be prepared to shuffle.

Arms Up

Now that your legs are set up and you know how to shuffle, let's look at what your arms should be doing. Simply put, they should be up and moving. Arms that are down by your sides give your opponent way too much room to move. You can distract her from her passing lanes by getting your arms out. Both arms should be stretched out about waist high, with your palms facing out and your fingers spread wide. This puts your arms in a ready position to rise up and block the ball if she shoots, or to tip or steal the ball if she tries to pass. Don't

"Uh-oh! Here Comes Spoon!"

I love being on defense. I adore it. I thrive on being on the defensive end and hounding someone the entire time. You're like a gnat. You get on their nerves. They want to hit you to get you off them. In their heads they're saying, "Uh-oh! Here comes Spoon!" When they get home, I want them to still see me. That's what I'm out to accomplish when I'm out on the court. That's what I always want, and that's what I always get.

stray too far away from the girl you are defending; you should be within arm's length most of the time so that you can reach her and the ball. If you know in advance that she is much quicker than you are, however, you might allow yourself a little extra space so that she won't be able to sprint by you.

"D" It Up

There are two basic categories of individual defense—when your opponent has the ball and when she doesn't. You need to be thinking about different things in each circumstance, but the bottom line is this: Defense wins games.

On-the-Ball Defense

When the person you are guarding is in possession of the ball, you need to be aware of whether she has used up her dribble. If she has, you can play close to try to shut off her options for what to do with the ball. Her triple-threat position has been reduced to two: pass or shoot. It is your job to make both of these as difficult as possible. But if she has not yet used her dribble when you pick her up with the ball, stay off enough to guard against her getting by you with a fake, a drive, or a screen from a teammate. As your girl starts to dribble, you want to stay between her and the basket at all times. You do this by shuffling with her and keeping your eyes on what she is going to do. The best plan is to watch her midsection. While she can fake you out by moving her head to one side or switching the direction of her feet, it is impossible for her to hide which way her hips are going to move. This is just a small secret to staying aware of where she is headed.

When your opponent is dribbling, keep your eyes on her midsection. This will keep you from being fooled by head fakes and fancy footwork. Her hips will always show the direction of her dribble.

Also, when she is dribbling, you want to make her path to the basket the longest it can be. Try to cut off the inside of the court so that she has to move around to the outside and thus stay farther away from the hoop. As she moves forward, you must utilize something to go backward rather than sideways, again so that you can move step-for-step with your opponent. This is known as a drop step, where your lead foot comes back a step and the other follows; again, be careful not to cross your legs. By executing a proper drop step, you will not lose your girl.

Defending the Top Gun

When I'm guarding the other team's best player, I start by taking a deep breath and telling myself, "Okay, don't be lazy." When you think of a great offensive player, like the Houston Comets' Cynthia Cooper, the Most Valuable Player in the WNBA for two years running, you really have to stay smart. You can't reach and you have to stay with your defensive fundamentals: moving your feet, having your hands active, and boxing out when the shot goes up.

Cynthia is very, very tough and she uses her picks well. When she comes off a pick, she knows whether she has the shot or the pass. She's absolutely a great offensive player. You have to think two or three steps ahead of what she's going to do. When I guard her I try to put as much pressure on her as I can, and when she gives the ball away I don't want to let her get it back.

Sometimes I'll tell the person I'm covering, "Even if you're going to the ladies' room, I'm going with you." That's the attitude you have to take when defending the top gun.

Off-the-Ball Defense

When the person you are defending does not have possession of the ball, your goal is to keep it that way. The key to do doing that starts with knowing where the ball is. If it is close enough to your girl that she can receive it in one pass, you need to stay pretty close to her, still in the proper stance that was discussed earlier. If the ball would take at least two passes to get to her, you have some room to play with and you don't have to be as close to her. But remember, if the ball moves to within one-pass range, you need to start closing in. When your girl doesn't have the ball, though, you are free to do some other things on the court to help out your team. Don't lose sight of her, and don't give her an open lane to cut to the basket and score an easy layup, either. But you can divide your attention somewhat.

One thing you can do is protect the part of the court known as the *key.* This is obviously the most dangerous area for the defense because it is where the other team can score the easiest baskets. You want to make that space as crowded as possible so it is more difficult

Play your opponent loose if she's away from the ball. Make sure, however, that you continuously keep track of where she is.

for opponents to get through to the hoop. When your girl is without the ball, try to keep the space around her well covered so it will be tough for one of her teammates to deliver it to her. If they try and your hands are well placed, you can pick off the ball before it reaches your girl and notch a steal. Sometimes that turns into an easy basket if you can drive down an open court for a layup. Or if your teammates are paying close attention, they can get out ahead of you; you can send the ball down the court and a fast-break basket is born.

Giving Help

Another important thing to do when your girl does not have the ball is to help out your teammates. If one of your teammates gets stopped by a pick and her girl is left open with the ball, you can use your shuffle step to guard that girl and stop her from scoring or making a good pass. The real key to helping out is communication. Good teammates talk to each other on the court. If you are aware that someone's girl is about to take a shot, yell out "Shot!" so your teammates will be ready to go for a rebound if she misses. If you notice one of your players has left the baseline open for a drive, yell "Baseline!" as a warning for her to pick it up. These are ways that one player can turn individual defense into a team effort. Be there for each other and be willing to help each other out. Never blame a teammate because the girl she was defending scored a basket. Be determined on the next possession to prevent it from happening again. There are many things that individual players can work on defensively, but if the five of you on the court are not working together, it won't do your team any good.

A *pick* or *screen* is when one player stands planted in a certain spot to block the path of an opposing player, thereby opening up a lane for her own teammate. Good teams will use screens very often on offense, and the opposing defense needs to be ready. The first option is to fight through it by anticipating its arrival and shuffling with your teammate past the screen. The next option would be to slide behind it, which is risky because you lose sight of the girl you are guarding; but if you can pick her up immediately after coming out of the screen, you should be okay. Use the slide when the girl setting the pick is too strong for you to fight through. The last option is to

Playing defense requires communication and making split-second adjustments. Be prepared to switch any time the player you are guarding sets a pick.

switch defensive assignments with a teammate, where you would pick up the girl who set the screen and your teammate would pick up your girl. This can be dangerous, though, if it results in size or speed mismatches. Finally, if it is your player who set the pick, you need to watch out for the roll.

The *pick-and-roll* is a very effective offensive weapon. It happens when the girl who set the pick is done with that job and has opened up a lane for her teammate. She then rolls quickly in the other direction and heads to the basket, where she hopes to receive a pass from the teammate she just helped out. If that girl is your defensive assignment, you have to stop her from getting open like that.

Defending the Post

Much of what we have looked at so far involves defense out on the perimeter, where guards do most of their work. Forwards and centers are usually in the key, and there are some other hints for learning how to defend the *low post*—the area under the basket. The closer you are to the hoop, the higher you should have your hands positioned. Don't raise both hands until your opponent shoots, however, because it is hard to move with grace and balance when both hands are above your head. But hold one hand high to at least help block the shooter's line of vision and path to the basket.

This positioning can make it possible for you to block a shot. If you think you can jump with your opponent, leap at the same time and swat the ball away before it gets into the cylinder above the net. Don't hit your opponents arm or you will be called for a foul. If you are taller than the girl who is taking the shot, you might be able to stop the shot without jumping—if you stuff it before she releases it. This could cause a turnover, and you should be ready to go for the ball. If you are not taller and can't jump as high as your opponent, be diligent by keeping a hand in the shooter's face and one above your

Live Up to Your Words

My biggest basketball thrill was the 1988 NCAA Championship game in which my team, Louisiana Tech, beat Auburn, 56–54. We were down sixteen at the half and Ruthie Bolton, now a star with the WNBA's Sacramento Monarchs, was on Auburn. She had one of her greatest halves ever, and I was guarding her. At halftime, my coach, Leon Barmore, pulled out the media guide in which I had mentioned that I loved to play defense. Then he said to me, "You're not doing it now!" In the second half I didn't let Ruthie score. She didn't get another point.

head to do your best to distract her effort. Then, once she releases the shot, turn and face the basket and box her out. This will put you in position to have first crack at the rebound if the shot misses.

Another defensive weapon while guarding the paint is to take a charge. When your opponent is driving to the hole, you are not allowed to jump in front of her to stop her, which would be a foul. But you can make yourself an obstacle for her by claiming you own piece of real estate. If she is coming, stand your ground and let her drive into you. If you have not moved your feet, she will be whistled for an offensive foul and your team will gain possession. There is no better satisfaction on defense than causing your opponent to make a mistake like that.

The element of surprise helps to confuse the opponent and cause turnovers.

Defense Drills

Let's look at a few drills that can help improve your defense. At least half of your practice time should be spent working on improving your defense.

Strengthen Your Quads

So much of defensive ability comes from having strong legs that are able to shuffle properly and stay low to the ground. The quadriceps muscles, the ones on the fronts of your thighs, are essential to this movement. Strengthen them by doing the skier squat, where you stand with your back to the wall and your feet about a foot away. Slide down the wall until your quadriceps are parallel to the ground and hold the position for twenty seconds.

Shuffle Drill

You need to practice the shuffle step to get comfortable with it. Start simply by shuffling from one side of the court to the other and back again. Also, practice moving backward as you shuffle, which you will need to do to execute the drop step. Increase your leg strength by getting into the defensive stance, running in place for a few steps, and then breaking into a shuffle. This simulates game conditions, during which you always want to be on the move.

Above all, remember that defense is not about glamour or headlines, it is about doing what it takes to win a basketball game. It is why I take so much pride in the fact that I was the WNBA's first-ever Defensive Player of the Year. It is why I led the league in steals, why I can sometimes smell a steal before it happens. Without defense, my game wouldn't be complete. And neither will yours.

Blaze's Thoughts

This is what Liberty general manager Carol "Blaze" Blazejowski thinks about my defense: "Spoon was the league's first-ever Defensive Player of the Year because she's quick, she anticipates well, she's tenacious and intense. It comes down to anticipation, whether you take a chance. A lot of times in our games, Teresa would double-down when the ball was inside and she would manage to grab it out of six or eight hands. Once in a while, when she takes a chance, you're going to lose with Teresa. You gamble and lose. But I'll take the odds, because she wins so much."

What Makes
a Team Player

When you make others around you better players, you are truly a team player. Basketball is a team game, and to be the best player you possibly can be you must be a team player. A good team player is unselfish. She praises her teammates and offers encouragement whenever needed. She is positive and supportive at all times. She always gives 100 percent, in every practice and game. She's upbeat and enthusiastic, and she has fun as she plays the game hard.

There's No *I* in Team

The best definition of *team player* is a girl who places team success ahead of individual achievement. Magic Johnson, Larry Bird, and Michael Jordan are three fine examples of great team players who stressed team goals rather than selfish play. Here are five things that make up a team player.

Thanks, Mr. Grunfeld

Knicks president and general manager, Ernie Grunfeld, admitted he didn't know what to expect from me before the Liberty's season began last year. After he saw me play, he said, "Everyone has their own style and obviously Teresa is very emotional. She's a high-intensity player who leaves it all out there on the floor. She has great leadership ability and she's a spark plug. The fans really relate to her. She has charm, she has charisma, and she plays with emotion and feeling. New York likes that. Seeing her play was a very pleasant surprise. I had never seen her play before, and I was very excited when I did see her. We're very happy that she's a Liberty player."

Be Focused

A team can't act as one without each player being completely focused. With everyone focused on one goal, everything will fall according to plan. I'm so focused during a game that you can just see it on my face. Sometimes I get so focused and excited about what I'm doing that the moment just sweeps me up. I'll just high-five the first row. Later on, I'll have no idea that I did that because I was just so consumed with the moment. This kind of behavior might look funny, or you might think I do it just to get the fans involved in the game. That may be partly true, but more importantly, my teammates see how much the game means to me and how much I want us to win. They know from my actions that I will do anything for them and anything for our team. And in turn, this motivates them.

Be Goal Oriented

You must have team goals. Don't get caught up with individual achievements. If you reach team goals, the individual accolades will come. You should work every day to help your team reach its goals. Our goal with the Liberty every year is to win the WNBA championship. Your individual goal should be to get better every day. You might want to make a list and write down the things that you wish to improve. For example, maybe you have a tendency to pick up your dribble when pressured and turn the ball over. Make it your goal to improve your ballhandling skills with each practice and game.

For example, my goal in my second season was to improve my shooting. During my first year in the WNBA, I didn't shoot very often. So every day in the off-season I worked on my shot at my gym in New York City. I played pickup games, mostly with guys. They would challenge me and say, "I'm not going to guard you, you never shoot." That really helped me achieve my goal. I became a better shooter.

The performance of each individual is crucial to the success of the team. Basketball is truly a team game, where individual success does not guarantee victory.

Accept Your Role

Let's say you were a star on a previous team, then you join a new team that has a lot of good players. How will you deal with that? Will you pout or complain? Can you accept the challenge of a supporting role, of having another person be the leading scorer? A team player does whatever is needed to make the squad better. And she does it without complaint.

Take the Liberty, for instance. We have a lot of good players, and there's a different person every night who can score twenty points for us. We know that and we accept our roles.

There must be no jealousy on a team, either. A jealous player is the rotten apple on the team. You must be happy, whether you are playing every minute of the game or just one minute. I've seen jealousy tear teams apart. If that happens, you have to address it immediately. That's something we as a team focus on avoiding. It doesn't matter who gets what. In the end, we all get the glory.

Be Willing to Work Together

Communication is the biggest key. Are you willing to listen to constructive criticism? Will you understand that a teammate is telling you something to make you a better player? You have to be able to work together, to be honest with each other and openly communicate. Criticism, if constructive, is about lifting, not pushing down. With the Liberty, we had meetings last year after games when each person said how they were feeling. Each person just opened up and let it out. We would bring all our thoughts together, learn from them, and start over. That was the key to coming back together after a bad game.

Toward the end of the WNBA's inaugural season, we went on a four-game losing streak. At the time we lost all the confidence that we had in ourselves, because everyone had different thoughts in their minds. We weren't focused on the same page. And so after a loss during that slide, we had a players-only meeting. We talked honestly to each other. We really regrouped and got things together after that, and we got our confidence back. That's what helped us reach the WNBA Championship game.

Us Instead of Me

This really says it all. The team is always first. How many minutes you get on the court don't matter. Make every minute count. I believe if you get a minute, you play a hard minute. People might say to me, "That's easy for you to say, since you played all the minutes your whole life." But that's not true. In 1987, I tried out for the Pan Am team and I didn't make it. But I didn't drop my head. Yes, my fire was dampened because I didn't make it, but I said to myself, "This won't happen to me again. Next time I get an opportunity to play on one of these teams if they only give me a minute, I'm going to bust my butt for that minute." The next year I made the Olympic team, and we won the gold medal.

Though some players are more gifted with talent than others, there are always times on the court when even a star is in need of her teammates.

The Crystal Ball

The future of women's basketball and the WNBA in this country is going to be huge. You have younger ladies now able to see what they can be by watching what's happening with us. They can see the emotion that we play with, the enthusiasm, the love, the joy that we have playing the game here in America. That emotion, joy, and enthusiasm is trickling down to them. Now they're just waiting for their turn. That's why I think it's going to be even greater as the years go on. You have kids now saying, "I can do this, too, let me just work at it." That's what we wanted to happen.

You can't imagine the joy we all feel about this league, even when we're not playing. The entire year, in every arena we go to, our mouths are wide open. Who would ever imagine walking into Madison Square Garden and seeing your picture up on the wall? I am a person who wants to continue to reach. I want to stay in awe. When I'm not in awe anymore, I'll be asking myself if I'm done.

8

Team Offense

Before we begin with the specifics of team offense, let's take a minute to go over the positions—the makeup of a basketball team on the floor. There are five players on the court at one time, and each position has a name as well as a number that coaches will often use to designate which one they are talking about.

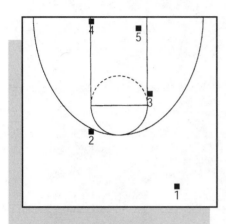

The basic offensive positions

Point guard (1): This is the player who controls the ball most of the time and is usually the team's best ball handler and decision maker. It is also usually a player who can drive, dribble, and pass equally well.

Shooting guard (2): Like the point guard, this is usually one of the smaller players, and together these two players make up a team's backcourt. Shooting guards are exactly what they sound like: shooters. The best pure shooter on the team is a natural for this position, one who can hit from the outside with consistency but can also deliver a good pass when needed (also called the *off-guard*).

The Point Is . . .

For as long I have been playing basketball, I have been my team's point guard. Playing the point, you have to be a leader. I am very vocal, and my teammates know that when I say something, I believe it. I believe in constructive criticism and in hugs. In bad times, I'll put my arms around my teammates and say, "I believe in you." In good times, I'll let my teammates know that they're great and get them to keep "handling their business." My teammates need to trust me as their playmaker, as their leader. Every day I'm out there, I'm proving that they can.

Small forward (3): Now we are moving into the frontcourt, which is usually reserved for the taller, bigger, and stronger players. Frontcourt warriors need to be physical enough to fight for rebounds and get inside position for layups, but they also need to be able to come out and hit short-range jump shots with consistency.

Power forward (4): Make the small forward stronger, taller, more physical, and you get a power forward. This type of player will play around the basket and in tandem with the center.

Center (5): Here's the big girl. Usually reserved for the team's tallest player, a center needs to be able to dominate the paint by scoring layups, boxing out, and rebounding; to be a complete player, she must also have the ability to send the ball back outside when options inside are cut off.

The center and power forward positions require players to post up (position themselves) near the basket. Lean into your defender with your body and use an arm to keep contact. Stretch your other arm out, signaling for a pass to be thrown to that side.

The Team Concept

Each player on the team must understand her role—scorer, passer, rebounder—and that she is only one part of a greater whole. The team must always come first, and each girl must do whatever it takes to help the team. Below are some keys to a successful team-oriented offense.

Don't Be Selfish

The first step in understanding team offense is that each of the five players on the floor has to be unselfish and willing to share the ball with her teammates. If one player wants to shoot all the time and make all the plays, it's not going to be difficult for the defense to figure out who is going to get the ball. Even if you score fifty points and the other team scores fifty-two, you lose. Being unselfish also means listening to your coach and following the coaching staff's strategy and philosophy.

Court Balance

When setting up on offense, you want to achieve court balance. Avoid having teammates bunched up too close to each other on the floor. Why? Well, for one thing, you make it too easy on the defense. If two of you are next to each other, you can be guarded by just one opponent, giving them a numbers advantage. Second, being too close together makes it impossible to pass to each other. You need to keep the court balanced by spreading yourselves out on offense, generally with the guards set up near the back of the halfcourt, the forwards more in the wings, and the center around the key. When your team is spread out properly, the defense must do the same thing, making it more difficult for them to trap you in bad situations. A good basketball team will flow on offense rather than getting clogged up. Court balance makes this possible.

Find the Open Girl

Now that your team is spread out properly, you will be able to see each other on the court and deliver smart passes. What makes a smart pass? Simply put, it's finding the open girl. You don't want to send the ball into traffic; it's too much of a risk for a turnover. Look for who has shed her defender and is ready to receive the ball. Making successive smart passes keeps the defense moving and can tire out the other team. When done right, you or one of your teammates will find yourself in position to take an open shot. Sometimes all it takes is a few passes to get the defense out of position. Another smart pass is one that gets to a teammate who is hot. If your shooting guard has just hit three jumpers in a row, you might want to find her again and take advantage of her streak.

Keep the Ball Moving

When you continue to make passes, the ball is never stationary. A moving target is much tougher to guard than one that is still. By getting the ball around to your teammates, everyone stays involved in the game and your offense is afforded many more options than if you all stand still with the ball. So keep the ball moving as much and as crisply as possible. Don't rush into a pass just because you want to get rid of the ball. Look for something that can lead to a basket. And just as you want to keep the ball moving, so, too, should you keep yourself moving, even if you don't have the ball. Make that *especially* if you don't have the ball. There is nothing more frustrating for a point guard trying to run an offense than watching her teammates stand around and wait to receive a pass. Make it easy for the point—get yourself open. Tire out the defense, make your defender work hard to guard you. Always remember, neither you nor the ball should be still. If you want to watch the game, sit on the bench or sit in the stands. If you want to play, get yourself moving.

Offensive players should be constantly moving—with or without the ball. Movement creates space for yourself, a teammate, or the ball handler.

Basketball for Lunch

Basketball is like food to me. I can't survive without it. Everywhere I turn in my New York hotel room, there are basketballs. I always have one in my hand. I even bring it to bed. I have to have it near me. I get emotional even when I think of stepping inside those four lines, and I think, "Now it's my turn to show you my talents. Now it's my turn to entertain." And when those moments are over, when forty minutes are done, I can't wait till the next time. I love to go to practice, too. I play and I practice like I'll never play or practice again. When I walk away, I'm beat. I'm dead tired. This game means so much to me. It's not a matter of life and death, but it means a lot. Where would *you* be without it?

Set Plays with Two Girls

Though we are talking about five players on the court at one time, some of the best set offensive plays can be run with just two players. For more than a decade, Karl Malone and John Stockton of the Utah Jazz have shown how two players who know each other's moves can break down a defense by themselves. I feel that I have the same chemistry with my teammate Vickie Johnson. Below are some two-girl set plays that cause problems for the defense.

The Pick-and-Roll

A simple but effective weapon, it begins when a player sets a screen for her teammate by blocking her defender. The teammate, who ends up free of her defender, can then drive to the basket. The player who set the pick then rolls the other way from the defender and finds herself free, also on the way to the basket.

The Give-and-Go

This play works when you pass the ball to your teammate, then shake your defender by faking a move away from the play. This will cause her to slack off just a little. When that happens, you reverse direction toward the basket, ready to receive a pass from the teammate you just gave the ball to.

The Backdoor Pass

If you watch the men's NCAA Tournament, you've seen the Princeton basketball team execute this play to perfection. The Tigers have made the backdoor pass popular again. It happens best when you can take advantage of a team trying to overplay the passing lanes. As you find yourself being pushed outside by your defender, you lean more that way, convincing her your path to the basket is safely cut off. But then you slip behind her and cut toward the hoop, with your hands raised and ready to catch a pass and score an open layup.

Using Picks and Screens

Earlier, I mentioned setting a screen for the pick-and-roll. We also looked at ways to stop this move when you are playing defense. So let's take some time to go over how to use a pick or screen on offense to help your team.

A good offensive team will set many picks and screens during a game, because they help you and your teammates get into some open space, and that's when you can create opportunities to score. *Setting a pick* happens when you plant your body in the path of a defender, thereby stopping her from being able to run with the teammate of yours that she is guarding. You do this by setting your body in a stationary position, with your feet perpendicular to the defender's. Make sure not to use your arms to block her, because that would be a foul. But you can keep them by your sides, or cross them over your chest close to your body.

When one teammate has set a pick, the recipient must make the best of it. To do this, cut by your teammate closely, shoulder to shoulder if you can, so that you make it impossible for your defender to follow you. When it works, you can create an open path to the basket. Or if that doesn't work, you can look for the teammate who set the screen to be rolling to the basket. It is a very fundamental play, but it is one that works well. It is predicated on unselfishness, however, a very important ingredient to success.

Once a pick has been set, fake to one side to get the defender's balance shifted that way. Then cut to the opposite direction, dribbling off the shoulder of your teammate.

Set Up the Offense

What forms does team offense take? Well, like setting up the defense, there are various ways to set up your offense. Sometimes the five players have specific spots they head to on the floor, and they work the ball around from those. When working against a *zone defense,* where each defender is covering an area of the floor, you try to move around your area to an open spot. Fake passes work well in this attack because they can get the defenders to move away from their players. Against a *player-to-player defense,* where each defender is covering a specific player, a good idea is to try to force the defense into an unbalanced situation. That can free up a player away from the bunch or can set up a good situation to use the pick-and-roll.

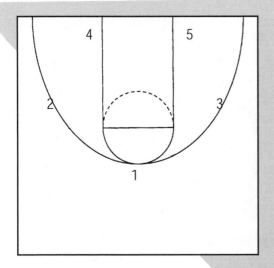

1-2-2 formation

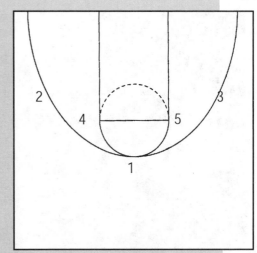

1-4 formation

Team offenses include setting up in formations like 1-2-2, 1-4, or 1-3-1. The point guard will have the responsibility of calling out which formation is to be used. She may decide herself what formation to call based on experience and instinct, or the formation may be called in from the coach on the bench. Your coach will give each offensive set a name that only your team will know, so the defense won't know what's coming.

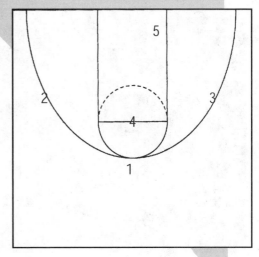

1-3-1 formation

Fast Break

Another common offensive sight in any basketball game is the *fast break.* To run a successful fast break, you need to have good, well-conditioned athletes who can make smart decisions in a split second. The fast break begins when your team gets possession in a way other than after the opposing team makes a basket. The most common way is on a rebound, but it could also be a steal or a loose ball.

When delivering the ball to a teammate in the post, make sure you pass it to a safe area. Throw the ball to the arm the player is signaling with. Her body will block the defender from intercepting the pass.

A good fast break starts with an outlet pass, which sends the ball out from under the basket to a waiting teammate. It will usually be a forward or center who makes the pass off a rebound, and it needs to be quick and strong. No need to drop the ball to your chest; it only wastes time. And don't dribble, because that will only give the defense time to set up or catch up. Passing is the quickest way to move the ball, and quickness is a most necessary element to the fast break. Make a one-handed throw that is strong and accurate. The receiver of the outlet pass will most likely be a guard, as she is the player who should be back near the foul line or midcourt. She then starts the fast break in the other direction, and if it is done quickly enough, she will already be ahead of the defense.

The guard must then decide whether to drive to the basket or pass to a teammate. The best choice is to take the ball toward the center of the court, to draw the defense in and allow your teammates to spread the fast-break offense. This will give you the option either to pass or shoot. The point is to get a quick, open shot, whether it is by you or your teammate doesn't matter. Teammates can make this possible by sprinting upcourt after the ball and filling the lanes on either side while the guard comes up the center. They then have the ability to cut to the basket for a layup. The prettiest fast break is the one where the ball never touches the floor, just travels from one pass to another all the way to the net.

A last thought on the fast break is for the teammates who start the play—the ones left behind while the fast break gets going. Don't stay where you are. Trail the play by sprinting up the court. Then, if the first shot falls and a rebound is tipped out, you are there to help keep the possession alive. Or if the defense caught up, you are there to bring the ball back out and let your team set up on offense. Remember, the fast break is a risky venture. You need to be smart and have a lot of basketball savvy. It looks great when you watch it on television, but it takes a lot of practice to make it look that easy.

Offense Drills

The best thing you and your friends can do is simulate a game. Practice what it feels like to be on the clock, playing under pressure. Set up situations that happen in a game. Practice the pick-and-roll, practice a two-on-one fast break.

Keep in mind that basketball is the ultimate team game led by great individual players. Unselfishness is so important that it can't be stressed enough. A good player is one who wants to make all her teammates on the court better.

Intensity

This is what my Liberty teammate Kym Hampton thinks about my game: "She puts the I in intensity. You open up the dictionary under intensity and there she is. If she can't get you pepped up, you're probably dead."

Three-Girl Weave

To understand how to fill the lanes on the fast break, try the three-girl weave. Three players should be spaced about fifteen feet apart. Start on the baseline. There is no dribbling in this drill. The player in the middle passes to a wing and then runs toward that player and behind her. The player who caught the pass throws it to the third player, running toward and behind her as well. Do this until you reach the far foul line, and then treat the situation like a fast break. Pass it to a teammate on the wing. That player shoots or drives.

9

Team Defense

To play great team defense, you must have great desire and be willing to give it your all. If your opponent goes out-of-bounds, you have to fall right out-of-bounds with her. To play good defense, you have to be in kind of a crazy state of mind; by that I mean you have to be intensely focused on good "D." Some things on defense can't be taught. You can't be taught to hustle. That's in you. Do you have it in you for forty minutes to really get after someone? That's where my tiger attitude comes in. I'm going to attack you all day long.

When the Liberty walk out on the court, the first thing we say in the huddle is: "Team defense!" That's what wins championships. The Liberty held our opposition to the league's lowest shooting percentage from the floor during the WNBA's inaugural season. Our defense is what brought us to the WNBA Championship game.

Before each game, tell yourself that it is going to be a defensive game. If your team plays good defense, your offense is going to work. Good defensive teams can beat more talented teams because their defense causes turnovers and forces their opponents to take poor shots. Also, you can always count on good defense. If your team's offense is off in a game, good defense will keep your team in it. That's why the best offense is good defense.

Be Proud

Pride means so much to me. I hate for someone to break down my pride. If an offensive player walks away with a smile on her face thinking, "Spoon couldn't guard me," I'm torn apart because that's where I want to be the best. I don't want her to walk off with a smile; I want her to walk off dead tired, thinking, "Oh, Spoon was everywhere." If someone beats me, I vow to work harder the next time.

Defense is about using your head and knowing your opponent. For example, does the player you are guarding always dribble to her right? Learn your opponent's tendencies and you'll play better defense. Is your girl quicker than you? If she is, give her enough room, because you want to be able to cover her if she makes a move to the basket. Is your player a good shooter? If she's in her range, play her close. What's your player's weakness? Is it that she can't dribble to her left? If so, move to her right side and force her to go left.

Man-to-Man

The two types of defense are man-to-man and zone. With man-to-man defense, you guard an opponent individually. You must stay with her at all times. If your girl has the ball, stay between her and the basket. If she does not have the ball, stay between her and the ball. Deny her the ball. Keep an eye on the ball, but don't lose track of your player. This is a good defense to use if your team is faster than your opponent's because you'll have an easier time keeping up

with your opponent. Man-to-man is also a good defense to use if your opponent is a good outside shooter. Stay with your opponent when she's away from the basket and try to block or prevent her outside shot.

Playing man-to-man defense is difficult when you're matched up against a player of exceptional talent.

Hold That Tiger

I love tigers, and I call myself a tiger on defense because tigers are never tame. I'm like that. I'll just keep coming at you. When I won the WNBA's Defensive Player of the Year award, I was like, "Wow!" The first thing I did was call my mom, and she wasn't surprised at all. She knows me well, knows how committed I am to good "D."

Defense is where I want to be the best. I want to guard the best, and I want to dictate the course of the game. You may think that it's the offense that controls the game while the defense just tries to contain it, but that attitude isn't going to win any games. I believe when I'm playing defense, I can make the game go my way. I don't have a cocky attitude; I'm not arrogant; I'm just very confident in my ability. I think everyone should be. I think once you step on the floor you should tell yourself, "I'm the best." And that's the way you'll play.

Zone

In zone defense, each defender covers an area of the court. When you're in your zone, you are ready to guard anyone who comes into your area. When a player comes into your zone, guard her as you would in a man-to-man defense until she leaves your area. The zone shifts as the ball moves from one offensive player to another, enabling the defense to stop the players who are the most threatening at that particular moment. Usually, when the ball isn't in your area, you sag into the lane to make it more difficult for your opponent to penetrate the zone.

The most common zone is the 2-3, which means that two players are up near the foul line and three are behind them, closer to the basket. Use this defense when you need good coverage out to the sides

Zone defenses make the game tough on dominant post players. Playing zone allows the defense to collapse in the paint and sometimes double- and triple-team dangerous players.

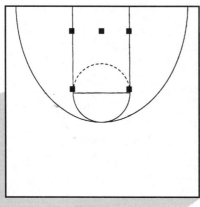

2-3 zone

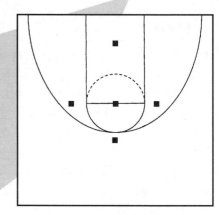

1-3-1 zone

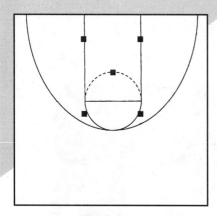

2-1-2 zone

of the basket. Other zones used frequently are the 1-3-1 and the 2-1-2. The 1-3-1 is best against a perimeter-oriented team because it clogs up shooting lanes and keeps players available to get in the opponents' faces. The 2-1-2 is for times when you want to clog up the paint and stop another team's post game. It works best against teams whose strongest players are in the frontcourt.

Zone Strengths

Zone defense can be a good way to stop an opponent's inside game. With five players packed in the paint, your opponents will have greater difficulty getting high-percentage shots. Zones are also effective when your opponent is a poor outside shooting team. If your team doesn't have to worry about your opponent's outside shot, your team can stay tight and shut down the area closer to the basket. Force teams to beat you from the outside. If you move well and keep the zone tight, opposing teams tend to get frustrated, then take a bad shot or force the ball into a crowd inside, often leading to a turnover.

Zones also are effective when your opponents are faster or taller than your teammates. If you are guarding a player in man-to-man and she is much faster than you are, then you won't be able to out-run her all the way to the basket. In zone defense, once that speedy player leaves your zone, your teammate takes over. If you are guarding a really tall girl, she can get her arms above yours to get a free shot. In the zone, your teammates are tightly guarding the area near the basket.

Zones work against impatient teams because teams often have to work the ball around to get a good shot against a zone. Zone defenses can also keep a player out of foul trouble: In a zone, the defensive responsibility isn't focused on one player, so a defender isn't likely to be prone to personal fouls. Zones can also establish good rebounding position. In the 2-3, for instance, the three players are stationed in good rebounding position.

Zone Weaknesses

The main weakness of playing zones is that gaps can occur on the borders of the zones, where players are uncertain sometimes about whose defensive responsibility it is. Also, a zone is not very effective against a good passing team, one that moves the ball quickly around the court. Against such movement, it's hard for the defense to shift quickly and the offense can just work the ball around until the "D" breaks down as players lose concentration or get tired.

The hardest part about learning a zone defense is moving as one unit. Remember the string concept: All five players should think of themselves as tied together so that they move as one and are aware of each other's movements.

The Press

The *press* is short for pressure. When your team runs a full-court press, you keep pressure on the offensive players in both the back-court and frontcourt. In the backcourt, the objective is to force a turnover, usually after a basket. On the inbounds pass, the pressing team swarms to the ball and to their opponent like ants to a picnic. If the opponent gets the ball past halfcourt, they have broken the press. The pressing team then falls back into their defense, whether it be man-to-man or zone.

The best time to use the full-court press is when your team is quicker and better-conditioned than the opposition. Many times a team will dribble the ball up the court slowly to catch a breather. By pressuring them, you can make them winded. If they get tired, they could commit costly turnovers. When your team is faster, they won't have trouble guarding the offensive players in the backcourt. Also, if a team has weak ballhandling skills, it might be easier to steal the ball in the backcourt before they get a chance in the frontcourt. The press is also commonly used when a team is behind and the final minutes are ticking down. Pressing can cause the other team to hurry and possibly panic with a turnover. Sometimes the press also helps teams break up the momentum of the game. If all your opponent's shots are falling and they have momentum, the press can disrupt their flow.

Double-teaming and trapping are also important elements of team defense. With a trap press, defenders double-team or trap a player using the sideline as a third defender. After an inbounds pass, two players trap the player who receives the pass. Two players swarm her and force her to the sideline. Don't give her an opportunity to look for an open teammate. Anticipate the desperation pass.

Communicate

Good defensive teams are good communicators. You can help your teammates by shouting "Help!" if your player gets by you, or "Shot!" when the ball is released, or "Pick right" or "Pick left" when a screen is being set. It helps keep everyone alert and prepares everyone for quick adjustments.

Team Defense Drills

Good team defense is a product of all five players being committed to stopping the other team from scoring. One weak link can break down the entire defense. Defense should be practiced as a team. Below are some drills you can practice with your squad.

The Teacher

Coach Barmore taught me the most about defense. He would always tell me to be aggressive. In high school, I was an offensive player. But Coach Barmore said, "If you can play defense, you can play on my team." I definitely wanted to be a part of his team. I was ready for the challenge. With him teaching me and constantly pushing me, I became the player I am today.

Good "D" Drill

Players pair off. One girl has the ball and dribbles from baseline to baseline in a zigzag motion. The defender gets into her defensive stance, shuffle-steps, and forces the dribbler to go the other way. When the offensive player goes to the right, the defender's left foot goes back and she shuffles to the left, and vice versa. The defender does not try to steal the ball, and the dribbler does not try to go past the defender. When the pair reaches the baseline, they switch roles and return.

After a walk-through, players should try it at half speed and then at full speed.

Here are a few tips for this drill. At full speed, the defender will likely be beat because she is shuffle-stepping, so the defender should turn and sprint to cut her off and head her off, then resume the defense stance and shuffle. The defender should try to force the dribbler to the sideline because the sideline acts as your friend, as a wall that makes your job easier.

Diagonal Drill

The defender lines up at the right corner, facing midcourt. She shuffle-steps toward the right end of the free-throw line. Her left leg should be in front. At that point she turns her hips, and heads to the opposite corner of the lane to face the baseline on a diagonal. There, she swings her hips again so that her right leg is now the lead leg of the shuffle-step. The player shuffle-steps to where the sideline is even with the free-throw line. The goal here is not speed, but form.

2-3 Zone Drill

In this drill, players react to passes. Put three offensive players on the perimeter and have them pass the ball to one another slowly. After each pass, the team should rotate. Pass again and the defense rotates, learning to act as one. Add a fourth player on offense to run the baseline. Finally, add a post player. The defense should not attempt steals. Instead, they should focus on reacting to the movement of the ball. Speed up the tempo after ten minutes.

10

Conditioning

Staying physically fit is one of the best ways to help your game. Even if you find yourself in a situation where you are matched up against more talented players, you can make a difference by being in better shape. You will be able to outrun your opponents to loose balls, get by the defense quicker, dribble by the offense faster, make sharper cuts to get open, and in general be a better athlete. You always need to improve your basketball skills, but don't ever forget you physical fitness, either.

The Off-Season

Let's talk first about the off-season. You still need to stay in playing shape even though the season is done. Without the grind of a game schedule, you can take advantage of the free time to fit longer workouts into your schedule. The first thing you should think about is a running regimen. In the off-season, two to three times a week is a good idea. Running on a treadmill is easy on the legs, and good if your knees need a break from the pounding of the road. But getting outside and breathing the fresh air is invigorating. If you're up for it, find a big hill and run up and down, which is a great way to strengthen your calf muscles. You can also go to any local field or track. Alternate turns running sprints or long distances, and if you find a football field, you can even mark off the distance of your sprint workouts. Remember the types of running that you do in basketball drills, and simulate them in your own workouts. Sprint ten yards, lifting your knees up high, then turn and go back, kicking your rear end.

Make sure, though, that you continue to follow a stretching regimen before and after any workout, whether it is during, before, or after the season. You never want to subject your muscles to a tough workout without getting them properly warmed up, or you will risk an injury.

If you haven't considered lifting weights, you may want to think about adding it to your regimen. I do a lot of lifting. It helps your endurance and your stamina. Don't worry, you're not going to get as huge as Hulk Hogan. There are ways to lift that will only define your muscles, not make them larger. Be sure to consult your coach or an expert before you start using weights. You can build up every area of your body, and all of it will add up to you being a better player.

Also, be aware of proper nutrition, which is really important. When your body is healthy, you will perform better. Talk to your parents or a nurse at school if you want advice about your diet. One easy thing to remember is to drink plenty of fluid when you are working out or when you are in a game. It keeps your body hydrated and your engine running. Also, get plenty of sleep and stay away from cigarettes, drugs, and alcohol.

In addition to the physical aspect of your off-season program, you should find time to analyze your game. Consider it mental calisthenics. Decide what areas you need improvement in. Make a plan to get better at those. If you can get videotapes of your games, watch them and try to determine what you can do to become a better player. Maybe you'll need to practice your left-handed dribbling, or moving when you don't have the ball, or even just shooting a lot so you become more accurate. The off-season is a great time to take advantage of the opportunity of figuring out ways to improve.

During the Season

The only real difference between physical workouts in the off-season and during your season is the amount of time you spend doing them. During the season, you should consider cutting down your weight-lifting sessions. I go from five times a week in the off-season to four times a week during the season.

When you are the best-conditioned athlete on the court, you will feel like you can be the last person standing when the game is over. If you're not in shape, you lose leg strength and you get too tired late in a game. You also lose concentration, which may not sound like it makes sense, but think about it. If you're tired late in the game, your mind will waste time worrying about being tired instead of focusing on the game. Conditioning plays a key role in having great endurance.

My Routine

I want to tell you about what I do during the season when I play for the Liberty. Lisa White, our team's trainer, is really great at working with us and keeping us in shape. Perhaps the biggest part of our routine is the weight lifting, because it helps establish and maintain strength in all of our muscles. I wouldn't recommend you really get serious about lifting weights until you are in high school, though, and then make sure you get supervised instruction on the proper way to use equipment. I started lifting weights in junior high, but that's mostly because of my brothers. They were always around the house flexing their muscles and lifting weights, and I just wanted to keep up with them. When I got to high school, and then college, at least I was ready for the weight training that became part of my commitment to playing basketball.

When you first go to a gym to learn about using weights, a good instructor will test you to find the maximum weight you can lift one time on each apparatus. You would take a percentage of that to figure out how much weight you should lift at the start. You would then do a certain number of repetitions at that percentage. For instance, if your best attempt at the leg press is one hundred pounds, you don't want to start with ten tries of one hundred pounds because you might hurt yourself or become overly fatigued. You might start instead at 70 percent, which means you would lift 70 pounds per repetition. Slowly, you can increase the weight per repetition. As Lisa warns us, if you try to do the reps at your maximum weight, you can strain your muscles. Also, you would be really sore and then would not be able to lift for a long time because of the time it takes for your body to recover. Then you would lose whatever progress you had gained by lifting the first time.

With the Liberty, each of the players has a personal routine for weight training and conditioning that we are expected to follow. On Mondays, we lift weights to strengthen muscles in our chests, triceps, and biceps (the front and back of the upper arm), and we do abdominal exercises. Exercises like the bench press can be used for the chest and can be done on a bench, with a bar, or with dumbbells. Lisa makes sure that we do at least three different exercises per body part. I think that younger players should do between eight and twelve repetitions per exercise. By repeating the exercise, you will gain strength.

Tuesday we work on our legs, lower backs, and abdomens. Leg exercises include the different muscles, like the quadriceps, hamstring, calf, and groin. You can do squats, leg presses, and leg extensions. Wednesday, we focus on our backs, shoulders, and abdomens. The reason we do abdominal exercises each time is that the muscles can handle it and recover every day and, if abdominal muscles are strong, there is less stress put on your back, which can prevent painful injuries. Other muscles need recovery time, which is why we rotate the areas we work on each day.

Thursday we take the day off from weights in preparation for Friday, when we do a total body workout. We hit each body part in the routine, doing fewer types of exercises per muscle. Friday's workout usually lasts about an hour, whereas on Monday, Tuesday, and Wednesday, the workout probably takes thirty to forty minutes. Of course, that doesn't include time spent talking to my teammates. So a lot of days the workouts take longer.

A few more pointers: One, on game days it is smarter to skip the weight training, because you don't want to be fatigued when the game starts. Two, consider getting a buddy for weight training. It can make it more fun to have someone to work out with, and the competition can push you both harder. And three, you should limit the time between each exercise to less than one minute, so that your body gets all the benefits of the workout.

We are not expected to do our weight training on weekends, but we continue to do aerobic exercise, which we also do during the week. That includes working out on the Stairmaster, a treadmill, or swimming. But like anything, start small and work your way up. One good idea is to get a monthly planner and chart each day with what you want to accomplish. It will enable you to see your goals in print and keep track of what you do.

NYPD Spoon

When we first got to New York, all the Liberty girls were together and out touring the city on an open-topped double-decker bus. At one point, we stopped by the harbor, where we had our picture taken with the Statue of Liberty in the background. A police boat pulled up near us in the water, and we told them who we were. They knew about our team, which still hadn't started its first season. I jumped on the boat and I almost killed my crazy self. I waved at the girls and took off. The cops were like, "Do you want to drive?" I said, "Sure." Vroom, vroom, and off I went.

The thing was, I couldn't control the boat. I nearly hit another boat. I asked them, "Please, take it back." So they took over and slowed it down. It was a crazy moment for me. My new teammates were like, "Spoon, you're nuts." Now they had an idea of what I was like.

The weirdest thing that happened to me was after I had made a public appearance in Brooklyn for the Police Athletic League. The police picked me up to take me home, but when we were nearly back to my hotel, they got a call that means another police officer was in danger. They were calm, but they turned the siren on and away we went. I figured it was a joke, but we went straight to a crime scene. I was in the backseat, so I ducked. If people saw me in the back of a police car, what would they think? They would have said, "What a role model she is." But it turned out that everything was okay. No one was in danger, but I was so nervous. That was real. Welcome to New York, Spoon!

Appendix

Teresa Weatherspoon's Playing Record

Louisiana Tech (1984–1988)

Career leader in steals (411) and assists (958)

Scored 1,087 career points and grabbed 533 career rebounds

Made two trips to the NCAA Finals

Won a national championship in 1988

Named to the 1987 and 1988 All-Final Four teams

Kodak All-America, 1987 and 1988

Louisiana State Player of the Year, 1988

Broderick Cup Winner, 1988

Wade Trophy Winner, 1988

Named to the NCAA Women's Basketball Team of the Decade for the 1980s

Professional Career (1988–present)

Teams in Italy include Busto (1988–1989 and 1990–1993), Magenta (1989–1990), and Como (1996–1997)

Played for Russian CSKA team (1993–1995)

Member of Italian League All-Star Team in 1996–1997

Led Busto in scoring (17.5 points per game) and rebounding (6.7 rebounds per game) in 1992

WNBA (1997)

Earned All-WNBA Second Team honors

Named the WNBA's Defensive Player of the Year

Led the league in both assists (6.1 per game) and steals (3.04 per game)

Started all 28 regular season games for the New York Liberty

Started both WNBA Playoff games and led the team with 37.5 minutes

WNBA (1998)

Earned All-WNBA Second Team honors for the second consecutive season

Named the WNBA's Defensive Player of the Year for the second consecutive season

Led the league in steals (3.33 per game)

Ranked second in assists (6.4 per game)

Other Highlights

Won an Olympic Gold Medal in 1988

Won a World Championship gold in 1986

Won Goodwill Games gold in 1986

Won World University Games gold in 1987

Won an Olympic Bronze Medal in 1992

Glossary

ABL	American Basketball League, a professional women's league.
Assist	A pass that results in a score by a teammate.
Backboard	The rectangular board from which the basket is suspended.
Backcourt	The half of the court containing the basket that a team is defending. After the offensive team enters its frontcourt, it's a violation to return to the backcourt with the ball.
Backdoor	A cut behind the defender to get open.
Bank shot	A shot attempt that uses the backboard.
Baseball pass	A long one-handed pass that is thrown with the same motion used to throw a baseball.
Baseline	The line on each end of the court that separates inbounds from out-of-bounds.
Basket	The goal that players shoot for to score points. Also, a shot that goes through the hoop.
Bounce pass	A pass that touches the floor before reaching its receiver.
Boxing out	Using the body to shield an opponent in order to gain a better position to grab a rebound.
Blocked shot	When a defensive player bats away or blocks an opponent's shot.
Breakaway	When a defensive player steals the ball and races toward her basket to score ahead of the defenders.
Carry	A violation committed when a player cradles the ball and holds it while dribbling.
Center	A position usually played by the tallest player on the team. A center scores near the basket, blocks shots, and does most of the rebounding.
Charge	A violation committed when an offensive player runs into a stationary defensive player.
Chest pass	A two-handed pass that is thrown from the player's chest to the chest area of the receiver.
Combination defense	A defense that combines zone and man-to-man.

Crossover	When a player changes hands while dribbling and moves away from the defender and toward the basket.
Cut	To move quickly from one spot on the floor to another in an effort to get open or beat a defender.
Defense	The team without the ball, who tries to keep the offensive team from scoring.
Double dribble	A violation in which a player dribbles the basketball with two hands at the same time.
Dribble	The bouncing movement of the ball. You may use either hand to dribble, but not both. You may switch hands while dribbling without stopping.
Drive	A quick offensive move to the basket by dribbling.
Dunk	To drive or stuff the ball through the basket from near or above the rim.
End line	See *Baseline*.
Fake	Using body movement to fool your opponent.
Fast break	A play in which the defense rebounds or recovers the ball after a steal and tries to advance the ball down the court quickly, ahead of the opponent, in hopes of an easy shot.
Field goal	All baskets are field goals except for free throws.
Forward	A position usually played by taller players. There are two forwards on a team.
Foul	A violation caused by illegal contact with an opponent; can result in free throws for an opponent.
Free throw	Also known as a foul shot. Awarded when a player on the opposing team commits a foul. Other players are not allowed to interfere with the foul shot, which counts for one point.
Free-throw lane	See *Key*.
Frontcourt	The half of the court with the basket where your team attempts to score. One team's frontcourt is the other's backcourt, and vice versa.
Full-court press	A defensive strategy in which the defense closely guards the offense in their backcourt and frontcourt.
Give-and-go	A play in which an offensive player passes to a teammate and cuts toward the basket, expecting a return pass.
Guard	A position usually played by small, quick players who are good ball handlers. There are two guards on a team. Also, to defend a play.
Half-court trap	When the ball handler is trapped in her backcourt by the sideline, defenders, and the midcourt line.

High post	A position around the free-throw line played by a forward or center.
Hook shot	A one-handed shot near the basket. The ball is thrown over the head in an arc toward the basket.
Hoop	Another name for the basket.
Inbounds pass	After a basket, or after some fouls, the ball is taken out-of-bounds and then passed back into play. When the ball is passed into play, it's called an inbounds pass.
Inside position	When a player is closer to the basket than her opponent.
Jump ball	Putting the ball into play by having an official toss it up between two opponents. The two players try to tap the ball to a teammate. At the start of the game, the jump ball is held at midcourt.
Jump shot	A shot in which the player jumps into the air and shoots at the same time.
Key	The area between the free-throw line and the baseline.
Lane	The area, usually painted, in front of each basket and below the free-throw line. Also called the paint.
Layup	A one-handed jump shot from one side of the basket, usually banked off the backboard.
Low post	The area nearest to the basket. A player who stands in that area is a low-post player.
Man-to-man defense	A type of defense in which a player has a specific player to defend.
Midcourt line	Divides the frontcourt from the backcourt.
NBA	National Basketball Association, a professional league.
NCAA	National Collegiate Athletic Association, comprised of colleges across the country. The NCAA tournament determines the national champion.
Offense	The team that has the ball.
One-and-one	A foul resulting in a player shooting one free throw and earning another if the first one is made.
Outlet pass	A pass made by a rebounder to a teammate to get the ball down the court quickly and trigger a fast break.
Overhead pass	A two-handed pass thrown from above the head.
Overtime	An extra period played when a game ends with a tie score.
Paint	See *Lane*.
Pass	Movement of the ball caused by a player's throwing it to another player.
Passing lane	The imagined path between a passer and her teammate.

Personal foul	Any player who holds, pushes, hits, or trips a player commits a personal foul. When a personal foul is called, the other team gets the ball.
Pick	A screen set by a teammate for the player with the ball.
Pick-and-roll	When an offensive player blocks a teammate's defender, then rolls toward the basket.
Pivot	When a player turns, or pivots, on one foot in order to change directions. The foot anchored to the ground is known as the pivot foot.
Point guard	The guard who primarily handles the ball and directs the offense.
Possession	When a team has the ball.
Post	The area outside the lane but near the basket.
Rebound	A missed shot that is retrieved.
Screen	A block by an offensive player set against a defender to free another offensive player for a shot or pass. Also called a *pick*.
Shoot	To throw the ball toward the basket to score.
Sideline	The lengthwise boundary of the court.
Square up	When a player turns her body toward the basket before shooting.
Strong side	The side of the court where the ball is located.
Substitute	To send a player in for another when play is stopped.
Taking a charge	A foul called against the offense when a defender plants herself in front of an opponent and the opponent runs into her.
Technical foul	A foul that does not necessarily involve contact with an opponent; includes unsportsmanlike contact or excessive time-outs.
Three-pointer	A shot made from outside the three-point arc.
Three seconds	A violation in which an offensive player remains in the paint for more than three consecutive seconds.
Time-out	Stoppage of play used to stop the clock or discuss strategy.
Tip-off	The start of a game by a jump ball.
Traveling	A violation in which a player walks or runs while holding the ball.
Trey	A three-pointer.
Turnover	A ballhandling error that gives the ball to the opposing team.
Weak side	The side of the court where the ball isn't.
WNBA	Women's National Basketball Association, a professional women's league.
Zone defense	The type of defense in which players guard a particular area of the court rather than a specific player.

Photo Credits

All photographs were taken by Michael Plunkett of Mountain Lion, Inc. Special thanks to the members of the girls basketball team at national powerhouse Christ the King High School in Queens, New York, for serving as our demonstrators.

Index